DEVOTIONS *for* LENT

New Living
Translation.
SECOND EDITION

TYNDALE HOUSE PUBLISHERS, INC.
CAROL STREAM, ILLINOIS

Visit Tyndale online at www.HolyBibleMosaic.com, www.newlivingtranslation.com, and www.tyndale.com.

Meditations and Introduction adapted from *Holy Bible: Mosaic*, copyright © 2009 by Credo Communications, LLC. All rights reserved.

Cover design by Rule29

Cover images: mosaic of Jesus Christ copyright © by Hazlan Abdul Hakim/iStockphoto; atlas and map of Roman empire copyright © by Duncan Walker/iStockphoto; ancient mosaic copyright © by Claudia Dewald/iStockphoto; holy book in light copyright © by Peter Zelei/iStockphoto; crown of thorns on grunge background copyright © by Jill Battaglia/iStockphoto; Tuscan texture, Bible, and mosaic tiles copyright © by iStockphoto. Cover and interior icon copyright © by Dover Publications. All rights reserved.

Devotions for Lent contains Scripture portions from the *Holy Bible*, New Living Translation.

Holy Bible, New Living Translation, copyright © 1996, 2004, 2007 by Tyndale House Foundation. All rights reserved.

This Bible is typeset in the typeface *Lucerna* designed by Brian Sooy & Co. exclusively for Tyndale House Publishers, Inc. All rights reserved.

TYNDALE, New Living Translation, NLT, and the New Living Translation logo are registered trademarks of Tyndale House Publishers, Inc. *The Truth Made Clear* is a trademark of Tyndale House Publishers, Inc.

ISBN 978-1-4143-3581-0

Printed in the United States of America

19 18 17 16 15 14 13
8   7   6   5   4   3   2

Tyndale House Publishers and Wycliffe Bible Translators share the vision for an understandable, accurate translation of the Bible for every person in the world. Each sale of the *Holy Bible*, New Living Translation, benefits Wycliffe Bible Translators. Wycliffe is working with partners around the world to accomplish Vision 2025—an initiative to start a Bible translation program in every language group that needs it by the year 2025.

Introduction

What is Lent? For some Christians, Lent has always been a part of their spiritual life and practice, but for others it is unfamiliar. Lent is the season when Christians have historically prepared their hearts for Easter with reflection, repentance, and prayer. Lent begins with Ash Wednesday and proceeds for forty days, culminating in Good Friday and Holy Saturday. Since Sundays are weekly celebrations of the resurrection of Jesus, the six Sundays in Lent are not counted as part of the forty-day season. Many Christians choose to fast throughout the season of Lent, but the focus is not so much on depriving themselves of something as it is on devoting themselves to God and his purposes in the world.

Lent is an important season of the church year. The church year is an excellent way to help us focus our attention on God by the way we organize our time. Rather than following the solar calendar's more familiar structure, organized by the rhythms of nature, the church calendar is organized around God and his activity in the world. The church calendar follows six seasons of varying length: Advent, Christmas, Epiphany, Lent, Easter, and Pentecost. Each of these seasons has a different focus: Advent focuses on the anticipation of God's coming into the world, both in the Incarnation and in Christ's second coming. Christmas concentrates on the birth of Christ. Epiphany centers itself in the light of God's presence shining in the world. Lent directs our attention toward human sin and God's gracious solution. Easter celebrates resurrection life. Pentecost helps us to remember and participate in the ongoing activity of the Holy Spirit in the world. The annual rhythm of these seasons can have a powerful effect on your personal and communal spiritual growth. More information about the church year and how it can shape your spiritual life can be found at www.HolyBibleMosaic.com.

Elements of Weekly Meditations

Each weekly meditation centers around a specific theme and uses several elements to create an environment for a meaningful experience with God. A brief introduction at the beginning of each weekly collection will start you on the path, and the remaining elements will help guide you along the way. This devotional will give you a taste of what is available throughout the year in *Holy Bible: Mosaic*.

Scripture. The first and most important element is the weekly listing of five Scripture readings. Four of these readings are adapted from standard lectionaries used by different Christian traditions around the world. These selections provide one reading each from the Gospels, the Psalms, the Old Testament, and the New Testament. The Suggested Reading is specifically chosen to complement the other readings in connection with the weekly theme.

Scripture is at the heart of each weekly meditation. Read these passages. Meditate on them. Read them again. Allow the text to penetrate your soul throughout the week as you engage with the other elements. Don't let the other elements eclipse the Scripture in your devotional time. They should complement the Scripture readings, not supersede them.

Historical and Global Contributions. One major distinctive of *Holy Bible: Mosaic* is the collection of reflective material from every continent and every century of Christian history. This material comes in many different forms that work together in each week's collection. You will find full-color artwork, excerpts from influential Christian thinkers throughout church history, quotes from brothers and sisters in Christ who have wrestled with ideas related to each week's theme, and worshipful pieces (including prayers, hymns, and poetry), all designed to bring you into contact with the global, historic church as you engage with God's Word.

Meditations. Each week also features an original meditation that connects the weekly theme to the modern world. These meditations were written specifically for *Holy Bible: Mosaic* by Christians engaged in living out the gospel in their own communities.

Whitespace. In addition to the lined spaces inviting you to write your thoughts down, ample space was purposefully given for you to draw, write, or interact with the material in any way that is helpful to you. Make use of the space however you want.

Ways to Use This Devotional

Individually. Use this Lent devotional in your personal devotional time, and allow the Scripture readings and meditative elements to serve as a springboard for your own prayer and reflections. Read the Scripture from the back of this booklet, or use your own Bible and see the readings in context.

In a Group. Families, Bible studies, and small groups can use this devotional to share in the experience together. Read the Scripture together, discuss the quotations and readings as a group, and talk about what God is doing in your lives through the Scripture and other material.

As a Church. If you are a church leader, consider using this devotional as a tool to encourage your entire congregation to read and reflect on Scripture throughout the season of Lent. Read the Scripture passages in your worship service, perhaps even preaching from one or more of them. This could be a great way for your church to share a communal devotional experience.

Any number of other ways might be imagined for using this book. Please feel free to share the unique ideas you have by e-mailing us at NLT@tyndale.com or by logging on to www.HolyBibleMosaic.com. There you will also find resources to extend the experience beyond the printed page, and you can add your piece to the Mosaic by contributing to the community forum or commenting on the blog.

Via Crucis—Pablo Sanaguano Sanchez (Ecuador/Contemporary)

Identifying Discontent

Lent, Week 1

GENESIS 2:15-17; 3:1-7 † P. 43 • PSALM 51 † P. 46
1 PETER 3:13-22 † P. 47 • MATTHEW 4:1-11 † P. 48

The season of Lent walks us through the grief of Jesus' last days before his crucifixion. As we read Jesus' personal conversation with his disciples in the upper room, we imagine the joy of friendship coupled with the sadness of a friend's imminent betrayal. As we enter into the darkness of Jesus' arrest, trial, and beating, we weep with those first Christians, and in our efforts to save Jesus from ourselves, we grieve in our Peter-like betrayals.

The tradition of Lent—a forty-day sacrifice—is one way of mourning the death that sin has caused in our lives. As we see Jesus perfectly withstand Satan's temptation in the wilderness, we admit our own shortcomings, our own inadequate sacrifices. This period of "giving up" has a profound way of recalling our desperate need for Jesus Christ.

SUGGESTED READING: GENESIS 2:4–3:24 † P. 43

"All God's plans have the mark of the cross on them, and all His plans have death to self in them." —E. M. BOUNDS (USA/1835–1913)

1816

1900 **JOHN CHARLES RYLE** (ENGLAND)

Remember what I say: if you would cleave to earthly pleasures, these are the things which murder souls. There is no surer way to get a seared conscience and a hard impenitent heart, than to give way to the desires of the flesh and mind. It seems nothing at first; but it tells in the long run.

Consider what Peter says: "abstain from fleshly lusts, which war against the soul" (1 Peter 2:11). They destroy the soul's peace, break down its strength, lead it into hard captivity, make it a slave.

Consider what Paul says: "Mortify therefore your members which are upon the earth" (Colossians 3:5). "And they that are Christ's have crucified the flesh with the affections and lusts" (Galatians 5:24). "But I keep under my body, and bring it into subjection" (1 Corinthians 9:27). Once the body was a perfect mansion of the soul; now it is all corrupt and disordered, and needs constant watching. It is a burden to the soul—not a helpmeet; a hindrance—not an assistance. It may become a useful servant, but it is always a bad master.

Consider, again, the words of Paul: "But put ye on the Lord Jesus Christ, and make not provision for the flesh, to fulfil the lusts thereof" (Romans 13:14). "These," says Leighton, "are the words, the very reading of which so wrought with Augustine, that from a licentious young man he turned a faithful servant of Jesus Christ."

People do not live by bread alone; rather, we live by every word that comes from the mouth of the LORD.
—**DEUTERONOMY 8:3**

"The Blood deals with what we have done, whereas the Cross deals with what we are. The Blood disposes of our sins, while the Cross strikes at the root of our capacity for sin." —**WATCHMAN NEE** (CHINA/1903–1972)

MEDITATION

AWE-FULL

Great and holy God
awe and reverence
fear and trembling
do not come easily to us
for we are not
Old Testament Jews
or Moses
or mystics
or sensitive enough.
Forgive us
for slouching into Your presence
with little expectation
and less awe
than we would eagerly give a visiting dignitary.
We need
neither Jehovah nor a buddy—
neither "the Great and Powerful Oz" nor "the man upstairs."
Help us
to want what we need . . .
You
God
and may the altar of our hearts
tremble with delight
at
Your visitation
amen.

—**FREDERICK OHLER** (USA/CONTEMPORARY)

Hollow Sacrifice

Eileen Button

Like many Catholic children, I gave up sweets for Lent. I remember creeping downstairs on Easter morning, hoping to be greeted by a marvelous chocolate bunny. After surviving the torturous season of sacrifice, I could barely wait to nibble the cottontail's long, delicious ears.

I would sometimes be disappointed to find a hollow chocolate cross in my basket instead. Propped in green plastic grass stood a milk chocolate version of my Savior's object of torture. I couldn't eat it. It felt blasphemous to do so. While it was almost impossible to endure the long, sweet-less days of Lent, the triviality of my "sacrifice" always shocked me when I was confronted by that chocolate cross on Easter morning.

The season of Lent is puzzling to many. Denying ourselves our favorite treats or habits—even for a short time—seems archaic in our I-want-it-now culture. Lent is a plodding, definitive crescendo that leads up to the cacophonous noise of Good Friday and the gorgeous aria of Easter. It's a season marked by deliberateness and intentionality.

But we often get in the way of our own best intentions. When fasting we might be tempted to feel a sense of pride about our sacrifice. The very thing we relinquish sometimes clamors inside us as a "need" to be met. Instead of focusing on Jesus Christ, our attention can dangerously be drawn to the very thing we've voluntarily surrendered.

Even so, the practice of Lent can be a valuable discipline. It's difficult to grasp what our sense of entitlement does to our bodies and souls. Our culture worships at the feet of pleasure. As we "shovel it in," we can become desensitized to our needs—the real hungers in our lives. Observing Lent can help us wrestle with the causes of our perpetual consumption. When we decide to relinquish what fails to truly satisfy, we come face-to-face with some tough questions. Can we believe Jesus when he says, "People do not live by bread alone, but by every word that comes from the mouth of God"? How can we make room for the Savior in our lives? Can we grasp the reality of Good Friday and live within its irony?

Lent challenges us to consider the honest answers to these and other soul-searching questions. It invites us to jump off the hamster wheel of consumption and experience the pinch of abstaining from thoughtless indulgence.

Perhaps I was offended by a hollow chocolate cross for another reason: The outside of our lives might look pretty, but we can be tragically empty. Occasionally, the reality of Jesus Christ's sacrifice and the power of his love break through our hardened hearts. The realization causes us to gasp. The hollow parts of our souls can be filled.

SHOW ME THE SUFFERING OF THE MOST MISERABLE

Show me the suffering of the most miserable;
So I will know my people's plight.
Free me to pray for others;
For you are present in every person.
Help me to take responsibility for my own life;
So that I can be free at last.
Give me honesty and patience;
So that I can work with other workers.
Bring forth song and celebration;
So that the Spirit will be alive among us.
Let the Spirit flourish and grow;
So that we will never tire of the struggle.
Let us remember those who have died for justice;
For they have given us life.
Help us love even those who hate us;
So we can change the world.
Amen.

—CÉSAR CHÁVEZ (USA/1927–1993)

REFLECTION

_____

_____

_____

_____

The sacrifice you desire is a broken spirit.
You will not reject a broken and repentant heart, O God.
—PSALM 51:17

Depression-era Farmer and Child—Ben Shahn (USA/1898–1969)

Dependence

Lent, Week 2

I t's no secret that our culture values independence. The iconic Lone Ranger is an American hero. But it doesn't take long before the Lone Ranger is dwelling in a pit of misery. Even the culture so entrenched in its I-can-do-it-myself attitude was quick to assume that the pronounced isolation of Seung-Hui Cho (the perpetrator of the 2007 Virginia Tech massacre) was the reason his severe unhappiness went unnoticed and ultimately led to tragedy.

From the very beginning of our faith story, Adam's loneliness is a sorrow to which all humanity can relate. Both God's creation of Eve for companionship and God's continued interference in human history by way of personal relationship shows that we were created to be relational beings.

While relationship doesn't demand the sacrifice of independence, it offers the gift of meeting our inadequacies. In such moments of weakness, we realize the strength of dependence.

SUGGESTED READING: ROMANS 4:1-25 † P. 51

"Christianity promises to make men free; it never promises to make them independent." —WILLIAM RALPH INGE (USA/1860–1964)

c. 365

435

JOHN CASSIAN (EGYPT)

This is something which has been handed on to us by some of the oldest of the Fathers and which we hand on to only a very small number of the souls eager to know it: To keep the thought of God always in your mind you must cling totally to this formula for piety: "Come to my help, O God; Lord, hurry to my rescue" [Psalm 70:1].

It is not without good reason that this verse has been chosen from the whole of Scripture as a device. It carries within it all the feelings of which human nature is capable. It can be adapted to every condition and can be usefully deployed against every temptation. It carries within it a cry of help to God in the face of every danger. It expresses the humility of a pious confession. It conveys the watchfulness born of unending worry and fear. It conveys a sense of our frailty, the assurance of being heard, the confidence in help that is always and everywhere present. Someone forever calling out to his protector is indeed very sure of having him close by. This is the voice filled with ardor of love and of charity. This is the terrified cry of someone who sees the snares of the enemy, the cry of someone besieged day and night and exclaiming that he cannot escape unless his protector comes to the rescue. . . .

This little verse, I am saying, proves to be necessary and useful to each one of us and, in all circumstances. For someone who needs help in all things is making clear that he requires the help of God not simply in hard and sad situations but equally and amid fortunate and joyful conditions. He knows that God saves us from adversity and makes our joys linger and that in neither situation can human frailty survive without His help.

MEDITATION

I CANNOT DO THIS ALONE

O God, early in the morning I cry to you.
Help me to pray
And to concentrate my thoughts on you;
I cannot do this alone.

In me there is darkness,
But with you there is light;
I am lonely, but you do not leave me;
I am feeble in heart, but with you there is help;
I am restless, but with you there is peace.
In me there is bitterness, but with you there is patience;
I do not understand your ways,
But you know the way for me. . . .

Restore me to liberty,
And enable me to live now
That I may answer before you and before men.
Lord, whatever this day may bring,
Your name be praised.
Amen.

—**DIETRICH BONHOEFFER** (GERMANY/1906–1945)

"No one is strong in his own strength, but he is safe by the grace and mercy of God." —**CYPRIAN** (TUNISIA/D. 258)

Lean on Me

Karen Sloan

"Lean on me." God makes this invitation to you and me in every moment of our lives. We can choose to respond, "Please, God, rescue me! Come quickly, Lord, and help me." But as for me, I often remain focused on myself. I become caught up either in all that I accomplish or in all that I have left undone. When life is all about me, I am blinded from the reality of my complete dependence upon my Creator. The noise of arrogance and anxiety deafens the call to lean on the everlasting arms.

We are designed by God to be doubly dependent. First, directly upon God, and second, indirectly upon God through those people God brings into our lives. Our existence is to be one of interconnection, not isolation.

As Jesus lived on earth as both God and man, he lived the ultimate life of continual dependence upon his Father; yet he also depended upon the provision from his Father through other people. God provided for Jesus' human life through Mary. Mary carried Jesus inside her body and in her arms. He received nourishment from Mary. She prepared his daily bread and mothered him with all her heart.

In adulthood, Jesus depended upon a community to accomplish the work he was called to do. A young boy provided the lunch that would feed five thousand. Jesus asked a woman for water at a well—and depended upon her word to evangelize her entire town, leading many to believe in him. When Jesus died on the cross, Mary was there with the other women and John, perhaps ready to hold his body one final time. Jesus called upon his disciple to do one more thing for him—take care of his mother. Even his tomb was a gift from one of his followers.

Yet Jesus did not stay in this tomb beyond three days. For the One he depended on before all others raised him from death to life.

There is freedom in dependence. It enables each of us to accept our vulnerability. We no longer have to hide in shame or self-sufficiency. You and I can choose to lean on our Father amid a full range of disastrous and delightful events, praying, "Please, God, rescue me! Come quickly, Lord, and help me."

Sixteen hundred years ago, John Cassian published an account of his conversations with monks living in a desert. One older monk, Isaac, had shared this prayer from Psalm 70 with John on his visit. Even today many Christians around the globe begin times of prayer with this verse. It serves as a clarion call to lean on God in the midst of our independent culture.

Dependence

— ✦ —

I look up to the mountains—
does my help come from there?
My help comes from the LORD,
who made heaven and earth!

—PSALM 121:1-2

REFLECTION

_____

_____

_____

_____

_____

_____

_____

_____

_____

_____

— ✦ —

If you try to hang on to your life, you will lose it.
But if you give up your life for my sake and for the
sake of the Good News, you will save it.

—MARK 8:35

WOMAN AT THE WELL—HATIGAMMANA UTTARANANDA (SRI LANKA/CONTEMPORARY)

God's Holiness and Grace

Lent, Week 3

Sometimes it's hard for us to get a solid grip on holiness. We're far removed from the Temple, which gave concrete expression to God's holiness. We don't have archived video of the Transfiguration, where Jesus revealed himself to his closest disciples. We lack tangible representations of holiness.

Still, is it possible that, like the saints before us, we can experience holiness? Maybe, more than we realize or care to admit, God's holiness is all around us. If that's the case, the implications could be vast.

If holiness is no longer a place in the Temple or a sacred ark, what is holiness? Where is holiness? And who is holy?

SUGGESTED READING: PSALM 11 † P. 56 • PSALM 93 † P. 57

---

*Holy, holy, holy is the LORD of Heaven's Armies!
The whole earth is filled with his glory!*
—ISAIAH 6:3

1886

1968

KARL BARTH (SWITZERLAND)

When we speak of grace, we think of the fact that [God's] favourable inclination towards the creature does not allow itself to be soured and frustrated by the resistance of the latter. When we speak of holiness, we think, on the other hand, of the fact that His favourable inclination overcomes and destroys this resistance.

To say grace is to say the forgiveness of sins; to say holiness, judgment upon sins. But since both reflect the love of God, how can there be the one without the other, forgiveness without judgment or judgment without forgiveness?

Only where God's love is not yet revealed, not yet or no longer believed, can there be here a separation instead of a distinction. In this case forgiveness would be inferred in abstracto from sin, and judgment from condemnation. It would not be God's judgment in the one case or God's forgiveness in the other.

If we speak in faith, and therefore in the light of God and His love, and therefore of God's forgiveness and judgment, as our insight grows we shall distinguish, but we shall certainly not separate, between God's grace and God's holiness.

The link between the two is decisively summed up in the fact that both characterise and distinguish His love and therefore Himself in His action in the covenant, as the Lord of the covenant between Himself and His creature.

For the sin of this one man, Adam, caused death to rule over many. But even greater is God's wonderful grace and his gift of righteousness, for all who receive it will live in triumph over sin and death through this one man, Jesus Christ.
—**ROMANS 5:17**

MEDITATION

PRAYER TO THE HOLY SPIRIT

Breathe in me,
O Holy Spirit,
that my thoughts may all be holy.

Act in me,
O Holy Spirit,
that my work, too, may be holy.

Draw my heart,
O Holy Spirit,
that I love only what is holy.

Strengthen me,
O Holy Spirit,
to defend all that is holy.

Guard me, then,
O Holy Spirit,
that I may always be holy.

—**AUGUSTINE OF HIPPO** (ALGERIA/354–430)

✠ Holy God

KEITH POTTER

In the season of Lent we remember the great sacrifice that Jesus Christ made, the forgiveness that was paid for with his life. We confess that our sins have gotten in the way of a relationship with God.

However, our confession will be thin and hollow unless we understand how great and holy God is. We are forever underestimating the seriousness of sin and its effects, making us unlike God and unfit for his good fellowship. Our efforts at forgiving ourselves and others will be thin and hollow as well unless we understand how God's grace so completely covers us through Jesus Christ, making us righteous in God's eyes and fit for his good fellowship.

So in this season, we meditate on God's holiness and wonder what it would be like to be filled only with loving intentions and healthy motivations, like our God.

In Isaiah 6, we discover that the story of the great prophet starts with a grand vision of God on his throne, surrounded by angelic beings. Day and night, these attendants cry out, "Holy, holy, holy is the LORD of Heaven's Armies! The whole earth is filled with his glory!" (Isaiah 6:3).

Isaiah's response?

"It's all over! I am doomed, for I am a sinful man. I have filthy lips, and I live among a people with filthy lips. Yet I have seen the King, the LORD of Heaven's Armies" (Isaiah 6:5).

Seeing God gave Isaiah eyes to see himself. Unclean. Badly acculturated in the filth of his surroundings. Anything but holy.

So God touched Isaiah. He enjoys forgiveness and cleansing and a new readiness. God calls out for a human agent.

Isaiah responds, "Lord, I'll go! Send me."

That can be our story. In light of God's holiness, we come undone. "Woe me! I'm an unclean person among unclean people. Now that I really see you, Lord, I see myself. Help!"

And God does help, with a grace greater than our sin. If his holiness is great, his grace is somehow overarching, for it covers every sin of ours that must offend the purity of his holiness. "Come, let us tell of the LORD's greatness; let us exalt his name together" (Psalm 34:3).

"He that sees the beauty of holiness, or true moral good, sees the greatest and most important thing in the world . . . Unless this is seen, nothing is seen that is worth the seeing; for there is no other true excellency or beauty." —JONATHAN EDWARDS (USA/1703–1758)

But the time is coming—indeed it's here now— when true worshipers will worship the Father in spirit and in truth. The Father is looking for those who will worship him that way. —JOHN 4:23

REFLECTION

_____

_____

_____

_____

_____

_____

_____

"What a contrast between God's character and ours! While human beings are disobedient and rebellious, God is gracious, merciful and loving." —YUSUFU TURAKI (NIGERIA/CONTEMPORARY)

Sin and Death

Lent, Week 4

NUMBERS 21:4-9 † P. 57 • PSALM 32 † P. 58
EPHESIANS 2:1-10 † P. 58 • JOHN 3:14-21 † P. 59

For some Christ-followers, sin and death weave so familiar a narrative that we've become numb to their sting. For others of us, the wages of sin and our subsequent spiritual death weigh so heavily that we refuse to accept God's gracious mercy.

The balance in which God calls us to rest is certainly dissatisfied with both extremes. As we begin to understand our current spiritual story through the eyes of Christian history, we grieve as we own the sins of humanity yet rejoice with the saints in the climax of our shared salvation story.

SUGGESTED READING: LUKE 15:1-32 † P. 59

---

*But God is so rich in mercy, and he loved us so much,
that even though we were dead because of our sins, he gave us life
when he raised Christ from the dead.*
—EPHESIANS 2:4-5

THE CRUCIFIED CHRIST—FRA ANGELICO (ITALY/C. 1395–1455)

1858

1922

PANDITA RAMABAI (INDIA)

Some years ago I was brought to the conviction that mine was only an intellectual belief—a belief in which there was no life. It looked for salvation in the future after death; and consequently my soul had not "passed from death unto life." God showed me how very dangerous my position was, and what a wretched and lost sinner I was; and how necessary it was for me to obtain salvation in the present, and not in some future time. I repented long; I became very restless and almost ill, and passed many sleepless nights. The Holy Spirit so got hold of me that I could not rest until I found salvation then and there. So I prayed earnestly to God to pardon my sins for the sake of Jesus Christ, and let me realize that I had really got salvation through Him. I believed God's promise, and took Him at His word; and when I had done this, my burden rolled away, and I realized that I was forgiven and was freed from the power of sin.

For God made Christ, who never sinned, to be the offering for our sin, so that we could be made right with God through Christ.
—**2 CORINTHIANS 5:21**

THE SACRIFICE

"O all ye who pass by, behold and see!"
Man stole the fruit; but I must climb the tree;
The tree of life to all, but only me:
  Was ever grief like mine?

    —**GEORGE HERBERT** (ENGLAND/1593–1633)

MEDITATION

PRAYER TO DO GOOD

Forgive me, most gracious Lord and Father, if this day I have done or said anything to increase the pain of the world. Pardon the unkind word, the impatient gesture, the hard and selfish deed, the failure to show sympathy and kindly help where I have had the opportunity, but missed it; and enable me so to live that I may daily do something to lessen the tide of human sorrow, and add to the sum of human happiness.

—F. B. MEYER (ENGLAND/1847–1929)

✛ The Smell of Sin

TIMOTHY G. WALTON

One early American preacher traveled from town to town preaching the gospel message. It was witnessed that as he approached the outskirts of a town, he would pause and say, "I smell hell!" If we were sensible to it, would the world smell like hell to us? Hell is an entirely foreign concept today. Yet that strange smell—the smell of decay, corruption, and filth—permeates this world we live in because of the aftermath of Adam and Eve's sin.

People have all kinds of creative ways of dealing with sin. They deny it. They minimize it. They make excuses for it. They blame others for it. The duke, a character in James Thurber's *The Thirteen Clocks*, admits, "We all have our little weaknesses; mine just happens to be that I am evil."

Why is sin *sinful*, not just a "little weakness"? Who says sin is *sin*? One of the words the Bible uses to refer to sin means "to miss the mark," implying that there is a mark or target that has been missed, so the word *sin* itself implies a standard. If a highway patrolman stops you for speeding, it implies that the official government has set a speed limit, and you violated it. Similarly, the moral standard for all humanity comes right out of the holy character of God. His glory, his holiness, is the standard we all fall short of.

This world that smells like sin also smells like death. The Bible says that "the wages of sin is death" (Romans 6:23). Sin leads to death. There was death in the Garden. Adam and Eve didn't drop dead the minute they ate the forbidden fruit, of course, but death made two instant inroads: First, the seed of physical death was planted in them. Two perfect individuals created to be forever young began to grow old and eventually would die. Second, they died spiritually. Their intimate and friendly relationship with the Lord died. The next scene in Genesis 3 finds Adam and Eve hiding from God in the bushes. Though they didn't realize it at the time, their only hope was for God to do something heroic to rescue them and bring them back into a healthy relationship with him. When God sacrificed two animals (Genesis 3:21) and proclaimed the coming of Jesus Christ, the Savior (Genesis 3:15), he did just that.

Modern life offers many luxurious "perfumes" to cover up the smell of eternal death. When we are enjoying our favorite foods and entertainments, it can be easy to forget the decay of sin and death all around us. Lent helps us to remember that there is only one who actually *reverses* decay—the God who raises the dead.

———

Yes, what joy for those
whose record the LORD has cleared of guilt,
whose lives are lived in complete honesty!
When I refused to confess my sin,
my body wasted away,
and I groaned all day long.
—PSALM 32:2-3

PRAYER FOR THE GRACE TO DIE DAILY

Grant, O Lord, that as we are baptized into the death of thy blessed Son our Saviour Jesus Christ, so by continual mortifying our corrupt affections we may be buried with him; and that through the grave and gate of death, we may pass to our joyful resurrection; for his merits, who died, and was buried, and rose again for us, thy Son Jesus Christ our Lord. *Amen.*

—BOOK OF COMMON PRAYER

REFLECTION

_____

_____

_____

_____

_____

"Therefore, O Faithful Christian, search for truth, hear truth, learn truth, love truth, speak the truth, hold the truth, defend the truth till death." —JAN HUS (BOHEMIA/C. 1369–1415)

Última Cena—Fray Gabriel Chavez and Jaime Domínguez Montes
(Mexico/Contemporary)

Fasting

Lent, Week 5

ISAIAH 58:1-12 † P. 61 • PSALM 130 † P. 63
ROMANS 8:6-11 † P. 63 • MATTHEW 6:1-21 † P. 63

For many Christians, it's customary to fast from some sort of pleasure or indulgence during Lent. When determining what to fast from, we often select something we perceive to be hindering growth in our relationship with Jesus Christ. But the most ancient forms of fasting—abstaining from food or observing a strict diet—were not done in an effort to remove sinful pleasures from one's life.

Perhaps in losing the art of fasting, we have lost the understanding about what can be gained from voluntarily giving up a presumed necessity. Throughout biblical and Christian history, many have fasted for reasonable and healthy periods. True, the expectations of instant gratification in our culture do not react well to the denial of nourishment. Could it be that God has something to reveal to us in the midst of our momentary self-denial?

SUGGESTED READING: ISAIAH 58:1-14 † P. 61

And when you fast, don't make it obvious, as the hypocrites do, for they try to look miserable and disheveled so people will admire them for their fasting. I tell you the truth, that is the only reward they will ever get. But when you fast, comb your hair and wash your face. Then no one will notice that you are fasting, except your Father, who knows what you do in private. And your Father, who sees everything, will reward you.

—MATTHEW 6:16-18

THE APOSTLES' TEACHING ON FASTING

But don't let your fasts be like the hypocrites. They fast on the second and fifth day of the week; but you should fast on the fourth day and the day of preparation (Friday). Also, don't pray like the hypocrites, but pray as the Lord commanded in his gospel: Our Father in heaven, may your name be kept holy. May your Kingdom come soon. May your will be done on earth, as it is in heaven. Give us today the food we need, and forgive us our sins as we have forgiven those who sin against us. And don't let us yield to temptation, but rescue us from the evil one. The power and the glory are yours forever. Pray in this way three times each day.

—**DIDACHE** (C. 90–180)

REFLECTION

_____

_____

_____

_____

_____

_____

_____

_____

_____

_____

"I can begin to see that Jesus expects us to fast not because He is
arbitrary or capricious or cruel, but because fasting does good work
on both our bodies and our souls."

—**LAUREN F. WINNER** (USA/CONTEMPORARY)

509

564

JOHN CALVIN (FRANCE)

Holy and lawful fasting has three objectives. We use it either to weaken and subdue the flesh that it might not act wantonly, or that we may be better prepared for prayers and holy meditations, or that it may be a testimony of our self-abasement before God when we wish to confess our guilt before him.

———

Moses remained there on the mountain with the LORD
*forty days and forty nights. In all that time he ate no bread and
drank no water. And the* LORD *wrote the terms of the covenant—
the Ten Commandments—on the stone tablets.*
—**EXODUS 34:28**

"Christians throughout history have fasted in preparation for the Lord's Supper. In addition to the elements of repentance and humility before God in this kind of fast, it is also intended to help the person focus on adoring the One who is represented in the Supper."
—**DONALD S. WHITNEY** (USA/CONTEMPORARY)

"Fasting is not confined to abstinence from eating and drinking. Fasting really means voluntary abstinence for a time from various necessities of life, such as food, drink, sleep, rest, association with people and so forth. The purpose of such abstinence . . . is to loosen to some degree the ties which bind us to the world of material things and our surroundings as a whole, in order that we may concentrate all our spiritual powers upon the unseen and eternal things."
—**OLE HALLESBY** (NORWAY/1879–1961)

✠ Purposeful Fasting

CLYDE TABER

Fasting is a strange word to our ears. We cringe, hesitate, and dismiss it. We sidestep it as gingerly as the religious leaders bypassed the beaten man in Jesus' parable. Yet fasting was part of the rhythm and flow of the life of the early church.

Jesus Christ affirmed and embraced the Old Covenant practice of fasting: "*When* you give to someone in need" (Matthew 6:2), "*when* you pray" (Matthew 6:5), "*when* you fast" (Matthew 6:16)—he taught all this on the Mount. Jesus assumed that giving, praying, and fasting were a normal part of the spiritual life. These are not electives, but part of the core teaching in the school of Christ.

Fasting preceded many great hinge points in human history. After Moses fasted, he received the tablets that changed our knowledge of sin and the world's sense of rightness (Exodus 34:28). After Jesus fasted, the cup began to flow with the wine of the New Covenant (Matthew 4:2). After the early church leaders fasted, the Jesus movement exploded beyond the borders of Palestine (Acts 13:2). The twentieth-century church in Asia fasted, and now it grows at unprecedented rates. The Father loves to reward those who fast with a pure heart (Matthew 6:18).

Fasting precedes purpose, and so purpose should precede fasting. When we fast, we should consider it a time of "setting aside" in order to "take up." We abstain from food for a time in order to better focus on Christ and his Kingdom. Fasting requires resolution and dedication. We take time to exit the highway of our busy lives. Fasting is most beneficial when accompanied with seeking, sacrificing, and sowing to the Spirit rather than the flesh. When we eat, we satisfy the flesh. When we fast, we reach beyond the flesh to the realm of the Spirit.

Fruitfulness in fasting is not quickly achieved. It is a practice that is enhanced with time and experience. When we enter into a season of fasting, the Lord gives grace. For a moment it reminds us of death, and then the Spirit translates the absence of food into a sense of life, light, and discernment.

As Jesus Christ was deliberate in his journey to Jerusalem, may we follow him in this practice. Not "*if* you fast," but "*when* you fast."

MEDITATION

DELIVER US FROM FEAR OF THE UNKNOWN

O Lord, we beseech thee to deliver us from the fear of the unknown future; from fear of failure; from fear of poverty; from fear of bereavement; from fear of loneliness; from fear of sickness and pain; from fear of age; and from fear of death. Help us, O Father, by thy grace to love and fear thee only, fill our hearts with cheerful courage and loving trust in thee; through our Lord and Master Jesus Christ.

—AKANU IBAIM (NIGERIA/1906–1995)

CLEANSING FLOW—VALERIE SJODIN (USA/CONTEMPORARY)

Hope

Passion Week

Isaiah 52:13–53:12 † p. 65 • Psalm 22 † p. 66
Philippians 2:5-11 † p. 68 • Luke 19:28-40 † p. 69

ope seems a strange bedfellow when paired with the likes of faith, love, and other paramount virtues. Hope is an expectation, a desire for fulfillment, but it only seems to make us anxious in the present. We hope for our dreams to be fulfilled, yet wonder what we will have left to hope in once they are. It almost seems cruel to tell friends that you love them, have faith in them, and have *hope* in them, as though they are not yet the friends you might like them to be.

And yet God assures us that we should faithfully place our hope in him. While it may seem a recipe for disappointment, as our earthly hopes most nearly always are, the virtue's classification with such noble aspirations as faith and love reminds us that God's promises are truly worthy of our deepest hope.

SUGGESTED READING: Mark 14:1–15:47 † p. 69

"Hope by its very nature captivates both our hearts and heads. It evokes deep emotion. It moves in and makes itself at home in our souls. It takes up residence at the very core of who we are. That is why it is so vital that we begin to place our hope in the Lord."

—**Adam R. Holz** (USA/CONTEMPORARY)

1903

1972

WATCHMAN NEE (CHINA)

God must bring us to a point—I cannot tell you how it will be, but he will do it—where, through a deep and dark experience, our natural power is touched and fundamentally weakened, so that we no longer dare trust ourselves. He has had to deal with some of us very strangely, and take us through difficult and painful ways, in order to get us there. . . . But then at last it is that he can begin to use us. . . .

We would like to have death and resurrection put together within one hour of each other. We cannot face the thought that God will keep us aside for so long a time; we cannot bear to wait. And of course I cannot tell you how long he will take, but in principle I think it is quite safe to say this, that there will be a definite period when he will keep you there. . . . All is in darkness, but it is only for a night. It must indeed be a full night; but that is all. Afterwards you will find that everything is given back to you in glorious resurrection; and nothing can measure the difference between what was before and what now is!

But I am a worm and not a man.
I am scorned and despised by all!
Everyone who sees me mocks me.
They sneer and shake their heads, saying,
"Is this the one who relies on the LORD?
Then let the LORD save him!
If the LORD loves him so much,
let the LORD rescue him!"
—PSALM 22:6-8

MEDITATION

Though he was God,
he did not think of equality with God
as something to cling to.
Instead, he gave up his divine privileges;
he took the humble position of a slave
and was born as a human being.
When he appeared in human form,
he humbled himself in obedience to God
and died a criminal's death on a cross.

—PHILIPPIANS 2:6-8

FOR STRENGTH

O God, the deathless hope of everyone, we rejoice that you support us both when young and even to old age. When our strength comes from you, it is strength indeed; but when our own strength is all we have, it is feebleness. You give refreshment and true strength.

—AUGUSTINE OF HIPPO (ALGERIA/354–430)

"We walk without fear, full of hope and courage and strength to do His will, waiting for the endless good which He is always giving as fast as He can get us able to take it in."

—GEORGE MacDONALD (SCOTLAND/1824–1905)

GIVE US GRACE

Lord God, whose blessed Son our Savior gave his body to be whipped and his face to be spit upon: Give us grace to accept joyfully the sufferings of the present time, confident of the glory that shall be revealed; through Jesus Christ your Son our Lord. —BOOK OF COMMON PRAYER

REFLECTION

✛ Saturday

STEVE THOMASON

Saturday was a long and dark day. Not only did the disciples hide in fear for their lives, but even worse, they grieved deeply. Soldiers had carried Jesus off to his execution the day before. Now their master was dead, and the grief cut deeply, leaving them utterly hollow.

They had not signed up for this. Jesus was supposed to lead them to victory over oppressors, establish a strong nation, and allow them to bask in the joy of sweet justice. Pain and grief were not part of the package.

Perhaps you have felt like the disciples that dark Saturday. I know I have. Over a fifteen-month period, I experienced the deaths of a friend, two grandmothers, my father-in-law, and the church that we had planted, along with some other close calls. It seemed like everything around me was dying. I thought following Jesus meant victory and peace. All I felt was pain and despair. I wish I could say that I handled it with poise and dignity. I didn't. I toggled between numb denial and irritating doubt. I wondered if I was to blame and God was punishing me for something. Perhaps I'd been duped and the universe really was a cold, empty place.

I have to think that the disciples had similar feelings on that dark Saturday, as if all hope was gone. We feel this way because we forget an important truth. The way of Jesus *is* a way of pain, grief, and sorrow. Jesus suffered much in his life—even before his arrest and execution. As a child he had to be hidden in Egypt in fear for his life. He wept over the death of his friend Lazarus. He grieved over the blindness of Israel. He agonized to the point of blood in the garden of Gethsemane. He screamed out as he hung on the cross, "My God, my God, why have you abandoned me?"

Jesus told us it would be this way. In Jesus' final teaching, he said that God would prune the branches that clung to the Vine (John 15:1-17). Pruning hurts. To have large parts of your life severed is not a pleasant experience. Yet, as the Gardener knows, without pruning there is no life.

That is the way of God's love and grace. God purifies us with pain. The disciples learned this and wrote to the churches about it. James said it is an opportunity for joy when troubles come because in the end it makes us complete. Peter told us that suffering refines our hearts like fire refines gold. Paul reached the climax of the whole process with one word—*hope*.

On Sunday the disciples became aware of a reality far deeper than Saturday's grief. They met hope. Jesus plowed through pain and grief and came out the other side. Saturdays will come, and they will be painful. But remember: without Saturday, we don't get Sunday. Jesus' love is our hope for today and forever. We *will* grieve, but with hope.

Scripture Readings

Lent, Week 1:
Identifying Discontent

GENESIS 2:4–3:24

This is the account of the creation of the heavens and the earth.

When the LORD God made the earth and the heavens, [5]neither wild plants nor grains were growing on the earth. For the LORD God had not yet sent rain to water the earth, and there were no people to cultivate the soil. [6]Instead, springs[1] came up from the ground and watered all the land. [7]Then the LORD God formed the man from the dust of the ground. He breathed the breath of life into the man's nostrils, and the man became a living person.

[8]Then the LORD God planted a garden in Eden in the east, and there he placed the man he had made. [9]The LORD God made all sorts of trees grow up from the ground—trees that were beautiful and that produced delicious fruit. In the middle of the garden he placed the tree of life and the tree of the knowledge of good and evil.

[10]A river flowed from the land of Eden, watering the garden and then dividing into four branches. [11]The first branch, called the Pishon, flowed around the entire land of Havilah, where gold is found. [12]The gold of that land is exceptionally pure; aromatic resin and onyx stone are also found there. [13]The second branch, called the Gihon, flowed around the entire land of Cush. [14]The third branch, called the Tigris, flowed east of the land of Asshur. The fourth branch is called the Euphrates.

[15]The LORD God placed the man in the Garden of Eden to tend and watch over it. [16]But the LORD God warned him, "You may freely eat the fruit

---

[1] 2:6 Or *mist.*

of every tree in the garden—¹⁷except the tree of the knowledge of good and evil. If you eat its fruit, you are sure to die."

¹⁸Then the LORD God said, "It is not good for the man to be alone. I will make a helper who is just right for him." ¹⁹So the LORD God formed from the ground all the wild animals and all the birds of the sky. He brought them to the man² to see what he would call them, and the man chose a name for each one. ²⁰He gave names to all the livestock, all the birds of the sky, and all the wild animals. But still there was no helper just right for him.

²¹So the LORD God caused the man to fall into a deep sleep. While the man slept, the LORD God took out one of the man's ribs³ and closed up the opening. ²²Then the LORD God made a woman from the rib, and he brought her to the man.

²³"At last!" the man exclaimed.

"This one is bone from my bone,
    and flesh from my flesh!
She will be called 'woman,'
    because she was taken from 'man.'"

²⁴This explains why a man leaves his father and mother and is joined to his wife, and the two are united into one.

²⁵Now the man and his wife were both naked, but they felt no shame.

³:¹The serpent was the shrewdest of all the wild animals the LORD God had made. One day he asked the woman, "Did God really say you must not eat the fruit from any of the trees in the garden?"

²"Of course we may eat fruit from the trees in the garden," the woman replied. ³"It's only the fruit from the tree in the middle of the garden that we are not allowed to eat. God said, 'You must not eat it or even touch it; if you do, you will die.'"

⁴"You won't die!" the serpent replied to the woman. ⁵"God knows that your eyes will be opened as soon as you eat it, and you will be like God, knowing both good and evil."

⁶The woman was convinced. She saw that the tree was beautiful and its fruit looked delicious, and she wanted the wisdom it would give her. So she took some of the fruit and ate it. Then she gave some to her husband, who was with her, and he ate it, too. ⁷At that moment their eyes were opened, and they suddenly felt shame at their nakedness. So they sewed fig leaves together to cover themselves.

⁸When the cool evening breezes were blowing, the man⁴ and his wife heard the LORD God walking about in the garden. So they hid from the LORD God among the trees. ⁹Then the LORD God called to the man, "Where are you?"

---

2 **2:19** Or *Adam,* and so throughout the chapter.
3 **2:21** Or *took a part of the man's side.*
4 **3:8** Or *Adam,* and so throughout the chapter.

[10]He replied, "I heard you walking in the garden, so I hid. I was afraid because I was naked."

[11]"Who told you that you were naked?" the LORD God asked. "Have you eaten from the tree whose fruit I commanded you not to eat?"

[12]The man replied, "It was the woman you gave me who gave me the fruit, and I ate it."

[13]Then the LORD God asked the woman, "What have you done?"

"The serpent deceived me," she replied. "That's why I ate it."

[14]Then the LORD God said to the serpent,

"Because you have done this, you are cursed
    more than all animals, domestic and wild.
You will crawl on your belly,
    groveling in the dust as long as you live.
[15] And I will cause hostility between you and the woman,
    and between your offspring and her offspring.
He will strike[5] your head,
    and you will strike his heel."

[16]Then he said to the woman,

"I will sharpen the pain of your pregnancy,
    and in pain you will give birth.
And you will desire to control your husband,
    but he will rule over you.[6]"

[17]And to the man he said,

"Since you listened to your wife and ate from the tree
    whose fruit I commanded you not to eat,
the ground is cursed because of you.
    All your life you will struggle to scratch a living from it.
[18] It will grow thorns and thistles for you,
    though you will eat of its grains.
[19] By the sweat of your brow
    will you have food to eat
until you return to the ground
    from which you were made.
For you were made from dust,
    and to dust you will return."

[20]Then the man—Adam—named his wife Eve, because she would be the mother of all who live.[7] [21]And the LORD God made clothing from animal skins for Adam and his wife.

---

[5] **3:15** Or *bruise;* also in 3:15b.

[6] **3:16** Or *And though you will have desire for your husband, / he will rule over you.*

[7] **3:20** *Eve* sounds like a Hebrew term that means "to give life."

[22]Then the LORD God said, "Look, the human beings[8] have become like us, knowing both good and evil. What if they reach out, take fruit from the tree of life, and eat it? Then they will live forever!" [23]So the LORD God banished them from the Garden of Eden, and he sent Adam out to cultivate the ground from which he had been made. [24]After sending them out, the LORD God stationed mighty cherubim to the east of the Garden of Eden. And he placed a flaming sword that flashed back and forth to guard the way to the tree of life.

PSALM 51

For the choir director: A psalm of David, regarding the time Nathan the prophet came to him after David had committed adultery with Bathsheba.

[1] Have mercy on me, O God,
     because of your unfailing love.
  Because of your great compassion,
     blot out the stain of my sins.
[2] Wash me clean from my guilt.
     Purify me from my sin.
[3] For I recognize my rebellion;
     it haunts me day and night.
[4] Against you, and you alone, have I sinned;
     I have done what is evil in your sight.
  You will be proved right in what you say,
     and your judgment against me is just.[9]
[5] For I was born a sinner—
     yes, from the moment my mother conceived me.
[6] But you desire honesty from the womb,[10]
     teaching me wisdom even there.

[7] Purify me from my sins,[11] and I will be clean;
     wash me, and I will be whiter than snow.
[8] Oh, give me back my joy again;
     you have broken me—
     now let me rejoice.
[9] Don't keep looking at my sins.
     Remove the stain of my guilt.
[10] Create in me a clean heart, O God.
     Renew a loyal spirit within me.
[11] Do not banish me from your presence,
     and don't take your Holy Spirit[12] from me.

---

[8] **3:22** Or *the man;* Hebrew reads *ha-adam.*
[9] **51:4** Greek version reads *and you will win your case in court.* Compare Rom 3:4.
[10] **51:6** Or *from the heart;* Hebrew reads *in the inward parts.*
[11] **51:7** Hebrew *Purify me with the hyssop branch.*
[12] **51:11** Or *your spirit of holiness.*

¹² Restore to me the joy of your salvation,
  and make me willing to obey you.
¹³ Then I will teach your ways to rebels,
  and they will return to you.
¹⁴ Forgive me for shedding blood, O God who saves;
  then I will joyfully sing of your forgiveness.
¹⁵ Unseal my lips, O Lord,
  that my mouth may praise you.

¹⁶ You do not desire a sacrifice, or I would offer one.
  You do not want a burnt offering.
¹⁷ The sacrifice you desire is a broken spirit.
  You will not reject a broken and repentant heart, O God.
¹⁸ Look with favor on Zion and help her;
  rebuild the walls of Jerusalem.
¹⁹ Then you will be pleased with sacrifices offered in the right spirit—
  with burnt offerings and whole burnt offerings.
  Then bulls will again be sacrificed on your altar.

1 PETER 3:13-22

Now, who will want to harm you if you are eager to do good? ¹⁴But even if you suffer for doing what is right, God will reward you for it. So don't worry or be afraid of their threats. ¹⁵Instead, you must worship Christ as Lord of your life. And if someone asks about your Christian hope, always be ready to explain it. ¹⁶But do this in a gentle and respectful way.[13] Keep your conscience clear. Then if people speak against you, they will be ashamed when they see what a good life you live because you belong to Christ. ¹⁷Remember, it is better to suffer for doing good, if that is what God wants, than to suffer for doing wrong!

¹⁸Christ suffered[14] for our sins once for all time. He never sinned, but he died for sinners to bring you safely home to God. He suffered physical death, but he was raised to life in the Spirit.[15]

¹⁹So he went and preached to the spirits in prison—²⁰those who disobeyed God long ago when God waited patiently while Noah was building his boat. Only eight people were saved from drowning in that terrible flood.[16] ²¹And that water is a picture of baptism, which now saves you, not by removing dirt from your body, but as a response to God from[17] a clean conscience. It is effective because of the resurrection of Jesus Christ.

²²Now Christ has gone to heaven. He is seated in the place of honor next to God, and all the angels and authorities and powers accept his authority.

---

[13] **3:16** Some English translations put this sentence in verse 15.
[14] **3:18a** Some manuscripts read *died*.
[15] **3:18b** Or *in spirit*.
[16] **3:20** Greek *saved through water*.
[17] **3:21** Or *as an appeal to God for*.

MATTHEW 4:1-11

Then Jesus was led by the Spirit into the wilderness to be tempted there by the devil. [2]For forty days and forty nights he fasted and became very hungry.

[3]During that time the devil[18] came and said to him, "If you are the Son of God, tell these stones to become loaves of bread."

[4]But Jesus told him, "No! The Scriptures say,

'People do not live by bread alone,
     but by every word that comes from the mouth of God.'[19]"

[5]Then the devil took him to the holy city, Jerusalem, to the highest point of the Temple, [6]and said, "If you are the Son of God, jump off! For the Scriptures say,

'He will order his angels to protect you.
And they will hold you up with their hands
     so you won't even hurt your foot on a stone.'[20]"

[7]Jesus responded, "The Scriptures also say, 'You must not test the LORD your God.'[21]"

[8]Next the devil took him to the peak of a very high mountain and showed him all the kingdoms of the world and their glory. [9]"I will give it all to you," he said, "if you will kneel down and worship me."

[10]"Get out of here, Satan," Jesus told him. "For the Scriptures say,

'You must worship the LORD your God
     and serve only him.'[22]"

[11]Then the devil went away, and angels came and took care of Jesus.

Lent, Week 2: Dependence

GENESIS 12:1-9

The LORD had said to Abram, "Leave your native country, your relatives, and your father's family, and go to the land that I will show you. [2]I will make you into a great nation. I will bless you and make you famous, and you will be a blessing to others. [3]I will bless those who bless you and curse those who treat you with contempt. All the families on earth will be blessed through you."

---

[18]**4:3** Greek *the tempter.*
[19]**4:4** Deut 8:3.
[20]**4:6** Ps 91:11-12.
[21]**4:7** Deut 6:16.
[22]**4:10** Deut 6:13.

⁴So Abram departed as the LORD had instructed, and Lot went with him. Abram was seventy-five years old when he left Haran. ⁵He took his wife, Sarai, his nephew Lot, and all his wealth—his livestock and all the people he had taken into his household at Haran—and headed for the land of Canaan. When they arrived in Canaan, ⁶Abram traveled through the land as far as Shechem. There he set up camp beside the oak of Moreh. At that time, the area was inhabited by Canaanites.

⁷Then the LORD appeared to Abram and said, "I will give this land to your descendants.²³" And Abram built an altar there and dedicated it to the LORD, who had appeared to him. ⁸After that, Abram traveled south and set up camp in the hill country, with Bethel to the west and Ai to the east. There he built another altar and dedicated it to the LORD, and he worshiped the LORD. ⁹Then Abram continued traveling south by stages toward the Negev.

PSALM 121

A song for pilgrims ascending to Jerusalem.

1 I look up to the mountains—
    does my help come from there?
2 My help comes from the LORD,
    who made heaven and earth!

3 He will not let you stumble;
    the one who watches over you will not slumber.
4 Indeed, he who watches over Israel
    never slumbers or sleeps.

5 The LORD himself watches over you!
    The LORD stands beside you as your protective shade.
6 The sun will not harm you by day,
    nor the moon at night.

7 The LORD keeps you from all harm
    and watches over your life.
8 The LORD keeps watch over you as you come and go,
    both now and forever.

PHILIPPIANS 3:12–4:1

I don't mean to say that I have already achieved these things or that I have already reached perfection. But I press on to possess that perfection for which Christ Jesus first possessed me. ¹³No, dear brothers and sisters, I have not achieved it,²⁴ but I focus on this one thing: Forgetting the past and looking

---

23 **12:7** Hebrew *seed.*
24 **3:13** Some manuscripts read *not yet achieved it.*

forward to what lies ahead, [14]I press on to reach the end of the race and receive the heavenly prize for which God, through Christ Jesus, is calling us.

[15]Let all who are spiritually mature agree on these things. If you disagree on some point, I believe God will make it plain to you. [16]But we must hold on to the progress we have already made.

[17]Dear brothers and sisters, pattern your lives after mine, and learn from those who follow our example. [18]For I have told you often before, and I say it again with tears in my eyes, that there are many whose conduct shows they are really enemies of the cross of Christ. [19]They are headed for destruction. Their god is their appetite, they brag about shameful things, and they think only about this life here on earth. [20]But we are citizens of heaven, where the Lord Jesus Christ lives. And we are eagerly waiting for him to return as our Savior. [21]He will take our weak mortal bodies and change them into glorious bodies like his own, using the same power with which he will bring everything under his control.

[4:1]Therefore, my dear brothers and sisters,[25] stay true to the Lord. I love you and long to see you, dear friends, for you are my joy and the crown I receive for my work.

MARK 8:31-38

Then Jesus began to tell them that the Son of Man[26] must suffer many terrible things and be rejected by the elders, the leading priests, and the teachers of religious law. He would be killed, but three days later he would rise from the dead. [32]As he talked about this openly with his disciples, Peter took him aside and began to reprimand him for saying such things.[27]

[33]Jesus turned around and looked at his disciples, then reprimanded Peter. "Get away from me, Satan!" he said. "You are seeing things merely from a human point of view, not from God's."

[34]Then, calling the crowd to join his disciples, he said, "If any of you wants to be my follower, you must turn from your selfish ways, take up your cross, and follow me. [35]If you try to hang on to your life, you will lose it. But if you give up your life for my sake and for the sake of the Good News, you will save it. [36]And what do you benefit if you gain the whole world but lose your own soul?[28] [37]Is anything worth more than your soul? [38]If anyone is ashamed of me and my message in these adulterous and sinful days, the Son of Man will be ashamed of that person when he returns in the glory of his Father with the holy angels."

---

[25] **4:1** Greek *brothers;* also in 4:8.
[26] **8:31** "Son of Man" is a title Jesus used for himself.
[27] **8:32** Or *began to correct him.*
[28] **8:36** Or *your self?* also in 8:37.

ROMANS 4:1-25

Abraham was, humanly speaking, the founder of our Jewish nation. What did he discover about being made right with God? [2]If his good deeds had made him acceptable to God, he would have had something to boast about. But that was not God's way. [3]For the Scriptures tell us, "Abraham believed God, and God counted him as righteous because of his faith."[29]

[4]When people work, their wages are not a gift, but something they have earned. [5]But people are counted as righteous, not because of their work, but because of their faith in God who forgives sinners. [6]David also spoke of this when he described the happiness of those who are declared righteous without working for it:

[7] "Oh, what joy for those
    whose disobedience is forgiven,
    whose sins are put out of sight.
[8] Yes, what joy for those
    whose record the LORD has cleared of sin."[30]

[9]Now, is this blessing only for the Jews, or is it also for uncircumcised Gentiles?[31] Well, we have been saying that Abraham was counted as righteous by God because of his faith. [10]But how did this happen? Was he counted as righteous only after he was circumcised, or was it before he was circumcised? Clearly, God accepted Abraham before he was circumcised!

[11]Circumcision was a sign that Abraham already had faith and that God had already accepted him and declared him to be righteous—even before he was circumcised. So Abraham is the spiritual father of those who have faith but have not been circumcised. They are counted as righteous because of their faith. [12]And Abraham is also the spiritual father of those who have been circumcised, but only if they have the same kind of faith Abraham had before he was circumcised.

[13]Clearly, God's promise to give the whole earth to Abraham and his descendants was based not on his obedience to God's law, but on a right relationship with God that comes by faith. [14]If God's promise is only for those who obey the law, then faith is not necessary and the promise is pointless. [15]For the law always brings punishment on those who try to obey it. (The only way to avoid breaking the law is to have no law to break!)

[16]So the promise is received by faith. It is given as a free gift. And we are all certain to receive it, whether or not we live according to the law of Moses, if we have faith like Abraham's. For Abraham is the father of all who believe. [17]That is what the Scriptures mean when God told him, "I have made you the father

---

[29] **4:3** Gen 15:6.
[30] **4:7-8** Ps 32:1-2 (Greek version).
[31] **4:9** Greek *is this blessing only for the circumcised, or is it also for the uncircumcised?*

of many nations."[32] This happened because Abraham believed in the God who brings the dead back to life and who creates new things out of nothing.

[18]Even when there was no reason for hope, Abraham kept hoping—believing that he would become the father of many nations. For God had said to him, "That's how many descendants you will have!"[33] [19]And Abraham's faith did not weaken, even though, at about 100 years of age, he figured his body was as good as dead—and so was Sarah's womb.

[20]Abraham never wavered in believing God's promise. In fact, his faith grew stronger, and in this he brought glory to God. [21]He was fully convinced that God is able to do whatever he promises. [22]And because of Abraham's faith, God counted him as righteous. [23]And when God counted him as righteous, it wasn't just for Abraham's benefit. It was recorded [24]for our benefit, too, assuring us that God will also count us as righteous if we believe in him, the one who raised Jesus our Lord from the dead. [25]He was handed over to die because of our sins, and he was raised to life to make us right with God.

Lent, Week 3:
God's Holiness and Grace

Exodus 17:1-7

At the LORD's command, the whole community of Israel left the wilderness of Sin[34] and moved from place to place. Eventually they camped at Rephidim, but there was no water there for the people to drink. [2]So once more the people complained against Moses. "Give us water to drink!" they demanded.

"Quiet!" Moses replied. "Why are you complaining against me? And why are you testing the LORD?"

[3]But tormented by thirst, they continued to argue with Moses. "Why did you bring us out of Egypt? Are you trying to kill us, our children, and our livestock with thirst?"

[4]Then Moses cried out to the LORD, "What should I do with these people? They are ready to stone me!"

[5]The LORD said to Moses, "Walk out in front of the people. Take your staff, the one you used when you struck the water of the Nile, and call some of the elders of Israel to join you. [6]I will stand before you on the rock at Mount Sinai.[35] Strike the rock, and water will come gushing out. Then the people will be able

---

[32] **4:17** Gen 17:5.
[33] **4:18** Gen 15:5.
[34] **17:1** The geographical name *Sin* is related to *Sinai* and should not be confused with the English word *sin*.
[35] **17:6** Hebrew *Horeb*, another name for Sinai.

to drink." So Moses struck the rock as he was told, and water gushed out as the elders looked on.

⁷Moses named the place Massah (which means "test") and Meribah (which means "arguing") because the people of Israel argued with Moses and tested the LORD by saying, "Is the LORD here with us or not?"

PSALM 95

¹ Come, let us sing to the LORD!
  Let us shout joyfully to the Rock of our salvation.
² Let us come to him with thanksgiving.
  Let us sing psalms of praise to him.
³ For the LORD is a great God,
  a great King above all gods.
⁴ He holds in his hands the depths of the earth
  and the mightiest mountains.
⁵ The sea belongs to him, for he made it.
  His hands formed the dry land, too.

⁶ Come, let us worship and bow down.
  Let us kneel before the LORD our maker,
⁷   for he is our God.
  We are the people he watches over,
    the flock under his care.

  If only you would listen to his voice today!
⁸ The LORD says, "Don't harden your hearts as Israel did at Meribah,
  as they did at Massah in the wilderness.
⁹ For there your ancestors tested and tried my patience,
  even though they saw everything I did.
¹⁰ For forty years I was angry with them, and I said,
  'They are a people whose hearts turn away from me.
  They refuse to do what I tell them.'
¹¹ So in my anger I took an oath:
  'They will never enter my place of rest.'"

ROMANS 5:1-21

Therefore, since we have been made right in God's sight by faith, we have peace with God because of what Jesus Christ our Lord has done for us. ²Because of our faith, Christ has brought us into this place of undeserved privilege where we now stand, and we confidently and joyfully look forward to sharing God's glory.

  ³We can rejoice, too, when we run into problems and trials, for we know that they help us develop endurance. ⁴And endurance develops strength of

character, and character strengthens our confident hope of salvation. [5]And this hope will not lead to disappointment. For we know how dearly God loves us, because he has given us the Holy Spirit to fill our hearts with his love.

[6]When we were utterly helpless, Christ came at just the right time and died for us sinners. [7]Now, most people would not be willing to die for an upright person, though someone might perhaps be willing to die for a person who is especially good. [8]But God showed his great love for us by sending Christ to die for us while we were still sinners. [9]And since we have been made right in God's sight by the blood of Christ, he will certainly save us from God's condemnation. [10]For since our friendship with God was restored by the death of his Son while we were still his enemies, we will certainly be saved through the life of his Son. [11]So now we can rejoice in our wonderful new relationship with God because our Lord Jesus Christ has made us friends of God.

[12]When Adam sinned, sin entered the world. Adam's sin brought death, so death spread to everyone, for everyone sinned. [13]Yes, people sinned even before the law was given. But it was not counted as sin because there was not yet any law to break. [14]Still, everyone died—from the time of Adam to the time of Moses—even those who did not disobey an explicit commandment of God, as Adam did. Now Adam is a symbol, a representation of Christ, who was yet to come. [15]But there is a great difference between Adam's sin and God's gracious gift. For the sin of this one man, Adam, brought death to many. But even greater is God's wonderful grace and his gift of forgiveness to many through this other man, Jesus Christ. [16]And the result of God's gracious gift is very different from the result of that one man's sin. For Adam's sin led to condemnation, but God's free gift leads to our being made right with God, even though we are guilty of many sins. [17]For the sin of this one man, Adam, caused death to rule over many. But even greater is God's wonderful grace and his gift of righteousness, for all who receive it will live in triumph over sin and death through this one man, Jesus Christ.

[18]Yes, Adam's one sin brings condemnation for everyone, but Christ's one act of righteousness brings a right relationship with God and new life for everyone. [19]Because one person disobeyed God, many became sinners. But because one other person obeyed God, many will be made righteous.

[20]God's law was given so that all people could see how sinful they were. But as people sinned more and more, God's wonderful grace became more abundant. [21]So just as sin ruled over all people and brought them to death, now God's wonderful grace rules instead, giving us right standing with God and resulting in eternal life through Jesus Christ our Lord.

JOHN 4:5-42

Eventually he came to the Samaritan village of Sychar, near the field that Jacob gave to his son Joseph. [6]Jacob's well was there; and Jesus, tired from the long walk, sat wearily beside the well about noontime. [7]Soon a Samaritan woman came to draw water, and Jesus said to her, "Please give me a drink." [8]He was alone at the time because his disciples had gone into the village to buy some food.

[9]The woman was surprised, for Jews refuse to have anything to do with Samaritans.[36] She said to Jesus, "You are a Jew, and I am a Samaritan woman. Why are you asking me for a drink?"

[10]Jesus replied, "If you only knew the gift God has for you and who you are speaking to, you would ask me, and I would give you living water."

[11]"But sir, you don't have a rope or a bucket," she said, "and this well is very deep. Where would you get this living water? [12]And besides, do you think you're greater than our ancestor Jacob, who gave us this well? How can you offer better water than he and his sons and his animals enjoyed?"

[13]Jesus replied, "Anyone who drinks this water will soon become thirsty again. [14]But those who drink the water I give will never be thirsty again. It becomes a fresh, bubbling spring within them, giving them eternal life."

[15]"Please, sir," the woman said, "give me this water! Then I'll never be thirsty again, and I won't have to come here to get water."

[16]"Go and get your husband," Jesus told her.

[17]"I don't have a husband," the woman replied.

Jesus said, "You're right! You don't have a husband—[18]for you have had five husbands, and you aren't even married to the man you're living with now. You certainly spoke the truth!"

[19]"Sir," the woman said, "you must be a prophet. [20]So tell me, why is it that you Jews insist that Jerusalem is the only place of worship, while we Samaritans claim it is here at Mount Gerizim,[37] where our ancestors worshiped?"

[21]Jesus replied, "Believe me, dear woman, the time is coming when it will no longer matter whether you worship the Father on this mountain or in Jerusalem. [22]You Samaritans know very little about the one you worship, while we Jews know all about him, for salvation comes through the Jews. [23]But the time is coming—indeed it's here now—when true worshipers will worship the Father in spirit and in truth. The Father is looking for those who will worship him that way. [24]For God is Spirit, so those who worship him must worship in spirit and in truth."

[25]The woman said, "I know the Messiah is coming—the one who is called Christ. When he comes, he will explain everything to us."

[26]Then Jesus told her, "I Am the Messiah!"[38]

[27]Just then his disciples came back. They were shocked to find him talking to a woman, but none of them had the nerve to ask, "What do you want with her?" or "Why are you talking to her?" [28]The woman left her water jar beside the well and ran back to the village, telling everyone, [29]"Come and see a man who told me everything I ever did! Could he possibly be the Messiah?" [30]So the people came streaming from the village to see him.

---

[36] **4:9** Some manuscripts do not include this sentence.

[37] **4:20** Greek *on this mountain.*

[38] **4:26** Or *"The 'I AM' is here"*; or *"I am the LORD"*; Greek reads *"I am, the one speaking to you."* See Exod 3:14.

[31]Meanwhile, the disciples were urging Jesus, "Rabbi, eat something."

[32]But Jesus replied, "I have a kind of food you know nothing about."

[33]"Did someone bring him food while we were gone?" the disciples asked each other.

[34]Then Jesus explained: "My nourishment comes from doing the will of God, who sent me, and from finishing his work. [35]You know the saying, 'Four months between planting and harvest.' But I say, wake up and look around. The fields are already ripe[39] for harvest. [36]The harvesters are paid good wages, and the fruit they harvest is people brought to eternal life. What joy awaits both the planter and the harvester alike! [37]You know the saying, 'One plants and another harvests.' And it's true. [38]I sent you to harvest where you didn't plant; others had already done the work, and now you will get to gather the harvest."

[39]Many Samaritans from the village believed in Jesus because the woman had said, "He told me everything I ever did!" [40]When they came out to see him, they begged him to stay in their village. So he stayed for two days, [41]long enough for many more to hear his message and believe. [42]Then they said to the woman, "Now we believe, not just because of what you told us, but because we have heard him ourselves. Now we know that he is indeed the Savior of the world."

PSALM 11

For the choir director: A psalm of David.

1 I trust in the LORD for protection.
   So why do you say to me,
      "Fly like a bird to the mountains for safety!
2 The wicked are stringing their bows
      and fitting their arrows on the bowstrings.
   They shoot from the shadows
      at those whose hearts are right.
3 The foundations of law and order have collapsed.
      What can the righteous do?"

4 But the LORD is in his holy Temple;
      the LORD still rules from heaven.
   He watches everyone closely,
      examining every person on earth.
5 The LORD examines both the righteous and the wicked.
      He hates those who love violence.
6 He will rain down blazing coals and burning sulfur on the wicked,
      punishing them with scorching winds.
7 For the righteous LORD loves justice.
      The virtuous will see his face.

---

[39]**4:35** Greek *white*.

PSALM 93

¹ The LORD is king! He is robed in majesty.
Indeed, the LORD is robed in majesty and armed with strength.
The world stands firm
and cannot be shaken.

² Your throne, O LORD, has stood from time immemorial.
You yourself are from the everlasting past.
³ The floods have risen up, O LORD.
The floods have roared like thunder;
the floods have lifted their pounding waves.
⁴ But mightier than the violent raging of the seas,
mightier than the breakers on the shore—
the LORD above is mightier than these!
⁵ Your royal laws cannot be changed.
Your reign, O LORD, is holy forever and ever.

Lent, Week 4: Sin and Death

NUMBERS 21:4-9

Then the people of Israel set out from Mount Hor, taking the road to the Red Sea[40] to go around the land of Edom. But the people grew impatient with the long journey, ⁵and they began to speak against God and Moses. "Why have you brought us out of Egypt to die here in the wilderness?" they complained. "There is nothing to eat here and nothing to drink. And we hate this horrible manna!"

⁶So the LORD sent poisonous snakes among the people, and many were bitten and died. ⁷Then the people came to Moses and cried out, "We have sinned by speaking against the LORD and against you. Pray that the LORD will take away the snakes." So Moses prayed for the people.

⁸Then the LORD told him, "Make a replica of a poisonous snake and attach it to a pole. All who are bitten will live if they simply look at it!" ⁹So Moses made a snake out of bronze and attached it to a pole. Then anyone who was bitten by a snake could look at the bronze snake and be healed!

---

[40] **21:4** Hebrew *sea of reeds.*

PSALM 32

A psalm[41] of David.

¹ Oh, what joy for those
 whose disobedience is forgiven,
  whose sin is put out of sight!
² Yes, what joy for those
 whose record the LORD has cleared of guilt,[42]
  whose lives are lived in complete honesty!
³ When I refused to confess my sin,
 my body wasted away,
  and I groaned all day long.
⁴ Day and night your hand of discipline was heavy on me.
 My strength evaporated like water in the summer heat.

 Interlude

⁵ Finally, I confessed all my sins to you
 and stopped trying to hide my guilt.
 I said to myself, "I will confess my rebellion to the LORD."
  And you forgave me! All my guilt is gone. *Interlude*

⁶ Therefore, let all the godly pray to you while there is still time,
 that they may not drown in the floodwaters of judgment.
⁷ For you are my hiding place;
 you protect me from trouble.
  You surround me with songs of victory. *Interlude*

⁸ The LORD says, "I will guide you along the best pathway for your life.
 I will advise you and watch over you.
⁹ Do not be like a senseless horse or mule
 that needs a bit and bridle to keep it under control."

¹⁰ Many sorrows come to the wicked,
 but unfailing love surrounds those who trust the LORD.
¹¹ So rejoice in the LORD and be glad, all you who obey him!
 Shout for joy, all you whose hearts are pure!

EPHESIANS 2:1-10

Once you were dead because of your disobedience and your many sins. ²You used to live in sin, just like the rest of the world, obeying the devil—the commander of the powers in the unseen world.[43] He is the spirit at work in the hearts of those who refuse to obey God. ³All of us used to live that way,

---

[41] **32:TITLE** Hebrew *maskil.* This may be a literary or musical term.
[42] **32:2** Greek version reads *of sin.* Compare Rom 4:7.
[43] **2:2** Greek *obeying the commander of the power of the air.*

following the passionate desires and inclinations of our sinful nature. By our very nature we were subject to God's anger, just like everyone else.

[4]But God is so rich in mercy, and he loved us so much, [5]that even though we were dead because of our sins, he gave us life when he raised Christ from the dead. (It is only by God's grace that you have been saved!) [6]For he raised us from the dead along with Christ and seated us with him in the heavenly realms because we are united with Christ Jesus. [7]So God can point to us in all future ages as examples of the incredible wealth of his grace and kindness toward us, as shown in all he has done for us who are united with Christ Jesus.

[8]God saved you by his grace when you believed. And you can't take credit for this; it is a gift from God. [9]Salvation is not a reward for the good things we have done, so none of us can boast about it. [10]For we are God's masterpiece. He has created us anew in Christ Jesus, so we can do the good things he planned for us long ago.

JOHN 3:14-21

"And as Moses lifted up the bronze snake on a pole in the wilderness, so the Son of Man must be lifted up, [15]so that everyone who believes in him will have eternal life.[44]

[16]"For God loved the world so much that he gave his one and only Son, so that everyone who believes in him will not perish but have eternal life. [17]God sent his Son into the world not to judge the world, but to save the world through him.

[18]"There is no judgment against anyone who believes in him. But anyone who does not believe in him has already been judged for not believing in God's one and only Son. [19]And the judgment is based on this fact: God's light came into the world, but people loved the darkness more than the light, for their actions were evil. [20]All who do evil hate the light and refuse to go near it for fear their sins will be exposed. [21]But those who do what is right come to the light so others can see that they are doing what God wants.[45]"

LUKE 15:1-32

Tax collectors and other notorious sinners often came to listen to Jesus teach. [2]This made the Pharisees and teachers of religious law complain that he was associating with such sinful people—even eating with them!

[3]So Jesus told them this story: [4]"If a man has a hundred sheep and one of them gets lost, what will he do? Won't he leave the ninety-nine others in the wilderness and go to search for the one that is lost until he finds it? [5]And when he has found it, he will joyfully carry it home on his shoulders. [6]When he arrives, he will call together his friends and neighbors, saying, 'Rejoice with

---

[44] 3:15 Or *everyone who believes will have eternal life in him.*
[45] 3:21 Or *can see God at work in what he is doing.*

me because I have found my lost sheep.' ⁷In the same way, there is more joy in heaven over one lost sinner who repents and returns to God than over ninety-nine others who are righteous and haven't strayed away!

⁸"Or suppose a woman has ten silver coins⁴⁶ and loses one. Won't she light a lamp and sweep the entire house and search carefully until she finds it? ⁹And when she finds it, she will call in her friends and neighbors and say, 'Rejoice with me because I have found my lost coin.' ¹⁰In the same way, there is joy in the presence of God's angels when even one sinner repents."

¹¹To illustrate the point further, Jesus told them this story: "A man had two sons. ¹²The younger son told his father, 'I want my share of your estate now before you die.' So his father agreed to divide his wealth between his sons.

¹³"A few days later this younger son packed all his belongings and moved to a distant land, and there he wasted all his money in wild living. ¹⁴About the time his money ran out, a great famine swept over the land, and he began to starve. ¹⁵He persuaded a local farmer to hire him, and the man sent him into his fields to feed the pigs. ¹⁶The young man became so hungry that even the pods he was feeding the pigs looked good to him. But no one gave him anything.

¹⁷"When he finally came to his senses, he said to himself, 'At home even the hired servants have food enough to spare, and here I am dying of hunger! ¹⁸I will go home to my father and say, "Father, I have sinned against both heaven and you, ¹⁹and I am no longer worthy of being called your son. Please take me on as a hired servant."'

²⁰"So he returned home to his father. And while he was still a long way off, his father saw him coming. Filled with love and compassion, he ran to his son, embraced him, and kissed him. ²¹His son said to him, 'Father, I have sinned against both heaven and you, and I am no longer worthy of being called your son.⁴⁷'

²²"But his father said to the servants, 'Quick! Bring the finest robe in the house and put it on him. Get a ring for his finger and sandals for his feet. ²³And kill the calf we have been fattening. We must celebrate with a feast, ²⁴for this son of mine was dead and has now returned to life. He was lost, but now he is found.' So the party began.

²⁵"Meanwhile, the older son was in the fields working. When he returned home, he heard music and dancing in the house, ²⁶and he asked one of the servants what was going on. ²⁷'Your brother is back,' he was told, 'and your father has killed the fattened calf. We are celebrating because of his safe return.'

²⁸"The older brother was angry and wouldn't go in. His father came out and begged him, ²⁹but he replied, 'All these years I've slaved for you and never once refused to do a single thing you told me to. And in all that time you never gave me even one young goat for a feast with my friends. ³⁰Yet when

---

⁴⁶ 15:8 Greek *ten drachmas*. A drachma was the equivalent of a full day's wage.

⁴⁷ 15:21 Some manuscripts add *Please take me on as a hired servant.*

this son of yours comes back after squandering your money on prostitutes, you celebrate by killing the fattened calf!'

³¹"His father said to him, 'Look, dear son, you have always stayed by me, and everything I have is yours. ³²We had to celebrate this happy day. For your brother was dead and has come back to life! He was lost, but now he is found!'"

Lent, Week 5: Fasting

ISAIAH 58:1-14

¹ "Shout with the voice of a trumpet blast.
   Shout aloud! Don't be timid.
Tell my people Israel[48] of their sins!
²   Yet they act so pious!
They come to the Temple every day
   and seem delighted to learn all about me.
They act like a righteous nation
   that would never abandon the laws of its God.
They ask me to take action on their behalf,
   pretending they want to be near me.
³ 'We have fasted before you!' they say.
   'Why aren't you impressed?
We have been very hard on ourselves,
   and you don't even notice it!'

"I will tell you why!" I respond.
   "It's because you are fasting to please yourselves.
Even while you fast,
   you keep oppressing your workers.
⁴ What good is fasting
   when you keep on fighting and quarreling?
This kind of fasting
   will never get you anywhere with me.
⁵ You humble yourselves
   by going through the motions of penance,
bowing your heads
   like reeds bending in the wind.
You dress in burlap
   and cover yourselves with ashes.

---

[48] **58:1** Hebrew *Jacob*. See note on 14:1.

Is this what you call fasting?
  Do you really think this will please the LORD?

[6] "No, this is the kind of fasting I want:
  Free those who are wrongly imprisoned;
    lighten the burden of those who work for you.
  Let the oppressed go free,
    and remove the chains that bind people.
[7] Share your food with the hungry,
    and give shelter to the homeless.
  Give clothes to those who need them,
    and do not hide from relatives who need your help.

[8] "Then your salvation will come like the dawn,
    and your wounds will quickly heal.
  Your godliness will lead you forward,
    and the glory of the LORD will protect you from behind.
[9] Then when you call, the LORD will answer.
    'Yes, I am here,' he will quickly reply.

"Remove the heavy yoke of oppression.
    Stop pointing your finger and spreading vicious rumors!
[10] Feed the hungry,
    and help those in trouble.
  Then your light will shine out from the darkness,
    and the darkness around you will be as bright as noon.
[11] The LORD will guide you continually,
    giving you water when you are dry
    and restoring your strength.
  You will be like a well-watered garden,
    like an ever-flowing spring.
[12] Some of you will rebuild the deserted ruins of your cities.
    Then you will be known as a rebuilder of walls
    and a restorer of homes.

[13] "Keep the Sabbath day holy.
    Don't pursue your own interests on that day,
  but enjoy the Sabbath
    and speak of it with delight as the LORD's holy day.
  Honor the Sabbath in everything you do on that day,
    and don't follow your own desires or talk idly.
[14] Then the LORD will be your delight.
    I will give you great honor
  and satisfy you with the inheritance I promised to your ancestor Jacob.
    I, the LORD, have spoken!"

PSALM 130

A song for pilgrims ascending to Jerusalem.

1 From the depths of despair, O LORD,
    I call for your help.
2 Hear my cry, O Lord.
    Pay attention to my prayer.

3 LORD, if you kept a record of our sins,
    who, O Lord, could ever survive?
4 But you offer forgiveness,
    that we might learn to fear you.

5 I am counting on the LORD;
    yes, I am counting on him.
    I have put my hope in his word.
6 I long for the Lord
    more than sentries long for the dawn,
    yes, more than sentries long for the dawn.

7 O Israel, hope in the LORD;
    for with the LORD there is unfailing love.
    His redemption overflows.
8 He himself will redeem Israel
    from every kind of sin.

ROMANS 8:6-11

So letting your sinful nature control your mind leads to death. But letting the Spirit control your mind leads to life and peace. 7For the sinful nature is always hostile to God. It never did obey God's laws, and it never will. 8That's why those who are still under the control of their sinful nature can never please God.

9But you are not controlled by your sinful nature. You are controlled by the Spirit if you have the Spirit of God living in you. (And remember that those who do not have the Spirit of Christ living in them do not belong to him at all.) 10And Christ lives within you, so even though your body will die because of sin, the Spirit gives you life[49] because you have been made right with God. 11The Spirit of God, who raised Jesus from the dead, lives in you. And just as God raised Christ Jesus from the dead, he will give life to your mortal bodies by this same Spirit living within you.

MATTHEW 6:1-21

"Watch out! Don't do your good deeds publicly, to be admired by others, for you will lose the reward from your Father in heaven. 2When you give to

---

[49] **8:10** Or *your spirit is alive.*

someone in need, don't do as the hypocrites do—blowing trumpets in the synagogues and streets to call attention to their acts of charity! I tell you the truth, they have received all the reward they will ever get. ³But when you give to someone in need, don't let your left hand know what your right hand is doing. ⁴Give your gifts in private, and your Father, who sees everything, will reward you.

⁵"When you pray, don't be like the hypocrites who love to pray publicly on street corners and in the synagogues where everyone can see them. I tell you the truth, that is all the reward they will ever get. ⁶But when you pray, go away by yourself, shut the door behind you, and pray to your Father in private. Then your Father, who sees everything, will reward you.

⁷"When you pray, don't babble on and on as people of other religions do. They think their prayers are answered merely by repeating their words again and again. ⁸Don't be like them, for your Father knows exactly what you need even before you ask him! ⁹Pray like this:

> Our Father in heaven,
>   may your name be kept holy.
> ¹⁰ May your Kingdom come soon.
>   May your will be done on earth,
>   as it is in heaven.
> ¹¹ Give us today the food we need,⁵⁰
> ¹² and forgive us our sins,
>   as we have forgiven those who sin against us.
> ¹³ And don't let us yield to temptation,⁵¹
>   but rescue us from the evil one.⁵²

¹⁴"If you forgive those who sin against you, your heavenly Father will forgive you. ¹⁵But if you refuse to forgive others, your Father will not forgive your sins.

¹⁶"And when you fast, don't make it obvious, as the hypocrites do, for they try to look miserable and disheveled so people will admire them for their fasting. I tell you the truth, that is the only reward they will ever get. ¹⁷But when you fast, comb your hair and wash your face. ¹⁸Then no one will notice that you are fasting, except your Father, who knows what you do in private. And your Father, who sees everything, will reward you.

¹⁹"Don't store up treasures here on earth, where moths eat them and rust destroys them, and where thieves break in and steal. ²⁰Store your treasures in heaven, where moths and rust cannot destroy, and thieves do not break in and steal. ²¹Wherever your treasure is, there the desires of your heart will also be.

---

⁵⁰**6:11** Or *Give us today our food for the day*; or *Give us today our food for tomorrow*.
⁵¹**6:13a** Or *And keep us from being tested.*
⁵²**6:13b** Or *from evil.* Some manuscripts add *For yours is the kingdom and the power and the glory forever. Amen.*

Passion Week: Hope

ISAIAH 52:13–53:12

¹³ See, my servant will prosper;
  he will be highly exalted.
¹⁴ But many were amazed when they saw him.[53]
  His face was so disfigured he seemed hardly human,
    and from his appearance, one would scarcely know he was a man.
¹⁵ And he will startle[54] many nations.
  Kings will stand speechless in his presence.
  For they will see what they had not been told;
    they will understand what they had not heard about.[55]

⁵³:¹Who has believed our message?
  To whom has the LORD revealed his powerful arm?
² My servant grew up in the LORD's presence like a tender green shoot,
  like a root in dry ground.
  There was nothing beautiful or majestic about his appearance,
    nothing to attract us to him.
³ He was despised and rejected—
  a man of sorrows, acquainted with deepest grief.
  We turned our backs on him and looked the other way.
    He was despised, and we did not care.

⁴ Yet it was our weaknesses he carried;
  it was our sorrows[56] that weighed him down.
  And we thought his troubles were a punishment from God,
    a punishment for his own sins!
⁵ But he was pierced for our rebellion,
  crushed for our sins.
  He was beaten so we could be whole.
  He was whipped so we could be healed.
⁶ All of us, like sheep, have strayed away.
  We have left God's paths to follow our own.
  Yet the LORD laid on him
    the sins of us all.

---

[53] **52:14** As in Syriac version; Hebrew reads *you*.

[54] **52:15a** Or *cleanse*.

[55] **52:15b** Greek version reads *Those who have never been told about him will see, / and those who have never heard of him will understand*. Compare Rom 15:21.

[56] **53:4** Or *Yet it was our sicknesses he carried; / it was our diseases*.

⁷ He was oppressed and treated harshly,
    yet he never said a word.
  He was led like a lamb to the slaughter.
    And as a sheep is silent before the shearers,
    he did not open his mouth.
⁸ Unjustly condemned,
    he was led away.[57]
  No one cared that he died without descendants,
    that his life was cut short in midstream.[58]
  But he was struck down
    for the rebellion of my people.
⁹ He had done no wrong
    and had never deceived anyone.
  But he was buried like a criminal;
    he was put in a rich man's grave.

¹⁰ But it was the LORD's good plan to crush him
    and cause him grief.
  Yet when his life is made an offering for sin,
    he will have many descendants.
  He will enjoy a long life,
    and the LORD's good plan will prosper in his hands.
¹¹ When he sees all that is accomplished by his anguish,
    he will be satisfied.
  And because of his experience,
    my righteous servant will make it possible
  for many to be counted righteous,
    for he will bear all their sins.
¹² I will give him the honors of a victorious soldier,
    because he exposed himself to death.
  He was counted among the rebels.
  He bore the sins of many and interceded for rebels.

PSALM 22

For the choir director: A psalm of David, to be sung to the tune "Doe of the Dawn."

¹ My God, my God, why have you abandoned me?
    Why are you so far away when I groan for help?
² Every day I call to you, my God, but you do not answer.
    Every night you hear my voice, but I find no relief.

---

[57] 53:8a Greek version reads *He was humiliated and received no justice.* Compare Acts 8:33.
[58] 53:8b Or *As for his contemporaries, / who cared that his life was cut short in midstream?* Greek version reads *Who can speak of his descendants? / For his life was taken from the earth.* Compare Acts 8:33.

³ Yet you are holy,
    enthroned on the praises of Israel.
⁴ Our ancestors trusted in you,
    and you rescued them.
⁵ They cried out to you and were saved.
    They trusted in you and were never disgraced.

⁶ But I am a worm and not a man.
    I am scorned and despised by all!
⁷ Everyone who sees me mocks me.
    They sneer and shake their heads, saying,
⁸ "Is this the one who relies on the LORD?
    Then let the LORD save him!
If the LORD loves him so much,
    let the LORD rescue him!"

⁹ Yet you brought me safely from my mother's womb
    and led me to trust you at my mother's breast.
¹⁰ I was thrust into your arms at my birth.
    You have been my God from the moment I was born.

¹¹ Do not stay so far from me,
    for trouble is near,
    and no one else can help me.
¹² My enemies surround me like a herd of bulls;
    fierce bulls of Bashan have hemmed me in!
¹³ Like lions they open their jaws against me,
    roaring and tearing into their prey.
¹⁴ My life is poured out like water,
    and all my bones are out of joint.
My heart is like wax,
    melting within me.
¹⁵ My strength has dried up like sunbaked clay.
    My tongue sticks to the roof of my mouth.
    You have laid me in the dust and left me for dead.
¹⁶ My enemies surround me like a pack of dogs;
    an evil gang closes in on me.
    They have pierced my hands and feet.
¹⁷ I can count all my bones.
    My enemies stare at me and gloat.
¹⁸ They divide my garments among themselves
    and throw dice[59] for my clothing.

¹⁹ O LORD, do not stay far away!
    You are my strength; come quickly to my aid!

---

[59] **22:18** Hebrew *cast lots.*

²⁰ Save me from the sword;
 spare my precious life from these dogs.
²¹ Snatch me from the lion's jaws
 and from the horns of these wild oxen.

²² I will proclaim your name to my brothers and sisters.⁶⁰
 I will praise you among your assembled people.
²³ Praise the LORD, all you who fear him!
 Honor him, all you descendants of Jacob!
 Show him reverence, all you descendants of Israel!
²⁴ For he has not ignored or belittled the suffering of the needy.
 He has not turned his back on them,
 but has listened to their cries for help.

²⁵ I will praise you in the great assembly.
 I will fulfill my vows in the presence of those who worship you.
²⁶ The poor will eat and be satisfied.
 All who seek the LORD will praise him.
 Their hearts will rejoice with everlasting joy.
²⁷ The whole earth will acknowledge the LORD and return to him.
 All the families of the nations will bow down before him.
²⁸ For royal power belongs to the LORD.
 He rules all the nations.

²⁹ Let the rich of the earth feast and worship.
 Bow before him, all who are mortal,
 all whose lives will end as dust.
³⁰ Our children will also serve him.
 Future generations will hear about the wonders of the Lord.
³¹ His righteous acts will be told to those not yet born.
 They will hear about everything he has done.

PHILIPPIANS 2:5-11

You must have the same attitude that Christ Jesus had.

⁶ Though he was God,⁶¹
 he did not think of equality with God
 as something to cling to.
⁷ Instead, he gave up his divine privileges⁶²;
 he took the humble position of a slave⁶³
 and was born as a human being.

---

⁶⁰ **22:22** Hebrew *my brothers.*
⁶¹ **2:6** Or *Being in the form of God.*
⁶² **2:7a** Greek *he emptied himself.*
⁶³ **2:7b** Or *the form of a slave.*

When he appeared in human form,[64]
8   he humbled himself in obedience to God
    and died a criminal's death on a cross.

9 Therefore, God elevated him to the place of highest honor
    and gave him the name above all other names,
10 that at the name of Jesus every knee should bow,
    in heaven and on earth and under the earth,
11 and every tongue confess that Jesus Christ is Lord,
    to the glory of God the Father.

LUKE 19:28-40

After telling this story, Jesus went on toward Jerusalem, walking ahead of his disciples. 29As he came to the towns of Bethphage and Bethany on the Mount of Olives, he sent two disciples ahead. 30"Go into that village over there," he told them. "As you enter it, you will see a young donkey tied there that no one has ever ridden. Untie it and bring it here. 31If anyone asks, 'Why are you untying that colt?' just say, 'The Lord needs it.'"

32So they went and found the colt, just as Jesus had said. 33And sure enough, as they were untying it, the owners asked them, "Why are you untying that colt?"

34And the disciples simply replied, "The Lord needs it." 35So they brought the colt to Jesus and threw their garments over it for him to ride on.

36As he rode along, the crowds spread out their garments on the road ahead of him. 37When he reached the place where the road started down the Mount of Olives, all of his followers began to shout and sing as they walked along, praising God for all the wonderful miracles they had seen.

38 "Blessings on the King who comes in the name of the LORD!
    Peace in heaven, and glory in highest heaven!"[65]

39But some of the Pharisees among the crowd said, "Teacher, rebuke your followers for saying things like that!"

40He replied, "If they kept quiet, the stones along the road would burst into cheers!"

MARK 14:1-15:47

It was now two days before Passover and the Festival of Unleavened Bread. The leading priests and the teachers of religious law were still looking for an opportunity to capture Jesus secretly and kill him. 2"But not during the Passover celebration," they agreed, "or the people may riot."

---

64 **2:7c** Some English translations put this phrase in verse 8.
65 **19:38** Pss 118:26; 148:1.

[3]Meanwhile, Jesus was in Bethany at the home of Simon, a man who had previously had leprosy. While he was eating,[66] a woman came in with a beautiful alabaster jar of expensive perfume made from essence of nard. She broke open the jar and poured the perfume over his head.

[4]Some of those at the table were indignant. "Why waste such expensive perfume?" they asked. [5]"It could have been sold for a year's wages[67] and the money given to the poor!" So they scolded her harshly.

[6]But Jesus replied, "Leave her alone. Why criticize her for doing such a good thing to me? [7]You will always have the poor among you, and you can help them whenever you want to. But you will not always have me. [8]She has done what she could and has anointed my body for burial ahead of time. [9]I tell you the truth, wherever the Good News is preached throughout the world, this woman's deed will be remembered and discussed."

[10]Then Judas Iscariot, one of the twelve disciples, went to the leading priests to arrange to betray Jesus to them. [11]They were delighted when they heard why he had come, and they promised to give him money. So he began looking for an opportunity to betray Jesus.

[12]On the first day of the Festival of Unleavened Bread, when the Passover lamb is sacrificed, Jesus' disciples asked him, "Where do you want us to go to prepare the Passover meal for you?"

[13]So Jesus sent two of them into Jerusalem with these instructions: "As you go into the city, a man carrying a pitcher of water will meet you. Follow him. [14]At the house he enters, say to the owner, 'The Teacher asks: Where is the guest room where I can eat the Passover meal with my disciples?' [15]He will take you upstairs to a large room that is already set up. That is where you should prepare our meal." [16]So the two disciples went into the city and found everything just as Jesus had said, and they prepared the Passover meal there.

[17]In the evening Jesus arrived with the twelve disciples.[68] [18]As they were at the table[69] eating, Jesus said, "I tell you the truth, one of you eating with me here will betray me."

[19]Greatly distressed, each one asked in turn, "Am I the one?"

[20]He replied, "It is one of you twelve who is eating from this bowl with me. [21]For the Son of Man[70] must die, as the Scriptures declared long ago. But how terrible it will be for the one who betrays him. It would be far better for that man if he had never been born!"

[22]As they were eating, Jesus took some bread and blessed it. Then he broke it in pieces and gave it to the disciples, saying, "Take it, for this is my body."

---

[66] **14:3** Or *reclining*.
[67] **14:5** Greek *for 300 denarii*. A denarius was equivalent to a laborer's full day's wage.
[68] **14:17** Greek *the Twelve*.
[69] **14:18** Or *As they reclined*.
[70] **14:21** "Son of Man" is a title Jesus used for himself.

²³And he took a cup of wine and gave thanks to God for it. He gave it to them, and they all drank from it. ²⁴And he said to them, "This is my blood, which confirms the covenant⁷¹ between God and his people. It is poured out as a sacrifice for many. ²⁵I tell you the truth, I will not drink wine again until the day I drink it new in the Kingdom of God."

²⁶Then they sang a hymn and went out to the Mount of Olives.

²⁷On the way, Jesus told them, "All of you will desert me. For the Scriptures say,

'God will strike⁷² the Shepherd,
   and the sheep will be scattered.'

²⁸But after I am raised from the dead, I will go ahead of you to Galilee and meet you there."

²⁹Peter said to him, "Even if everyone else deserts you, I never will."

³⁰Jesus replied, "I tell you the truth, Peter—this very night, before the rooster crows twice, you will deny three times that you even know me."

³¹"No!" Peter declared emphatically. "Even if I have to die with you, I will never deny you!" And all the others vowed the same.

³²They went to the olive grove called Gethsemane, and Jesus said, "Sit here while I go and pray." ³³He took Peter, James, and John with him, and he became deeply troubled and distressed. ³⁴He told them, "My soul is crushed with grief to the point of death. Stay here and keep watch with me."

³⁵He went on a little farther and fell to the ground. He prayed that, if it were possible, the awful hour awaiting him might pass by. ³⁶"Abba, Father,"⁷³ he cried out, "everything is possible for you. Please take this cup of suffering away from me. Yet I want your will to be done, not mine."

³⁷Then he returned and found the disciples asleep. He said to Peter, "Simon, are you asleep? Couldn't you watch with me even one hour? ³⁸Keep watch and pray, so that you will not give in to temptation. For the spirit is willing, but the body is weak."

³⁹Then Jesus left them again and prayed the same prayer as before. ⁴⁰When he returned to them again, he found them sleeping, for they couldn't keep their eyes open. And they didn't know what to say.

⁴¹When he returned to them the third time, he said, "Go ahead and sleep. Have your rest. But no—the time has come. The Son of Man is betrayed into the hands of sinners. ⁴²Up, let's be going. Look, my betrayer is here!"

⁴³And immediately, even as Jesus said this, Judas, one of the twelve disciples, arrived with a crowd of men armed with swords and clubs. They had been sent by the leading priests, the teachers of religious law, and the elders. ⁴⁴The traitor, Judas, had given them a prearranged signal: "You will know which one to arrest when I greet him with a kiss. Then you can take him away

---

⁷¹ **14:24** Some manuscripts read *the new covenant.*
⁷² **14:27** Greek *I will strike.* Zech 13:7.
⁷³ **14:36** *Abba* is an Aramaic term for "father."

under guard." ⁴⁵As soon as they arrived, Judas walked up to Jesus. "Rabbi!" he exclaimed, and gave him the kiss.

⁴⁶Then the others grabbed Jesus and arrested him. ⁴⁷But one of the men with Jesus pulled out his sword and struck the high priest's slave, slashing off his ear.

⁴⁸Jesus asked them, "Am I some dangerous revolutionary, that you come with swords and clubs to arrest me? ⁴⁹Why didn't you arrest me in the Temple? I was there among you teaching every day. But these things are happening to fulfill what the Scriptures say about me."

⁵⁰Then all his disciples deserted him and ran away. ⁵¹One young man following behind was clothed only in a long linen shirt. When the mob tried to grab him, ⁵²he slipped out of his shirt and ran away naked.

⁵³They took Jesus to the high priest's home where the leading priests, the elders, and the teachers of religious law had gathered. ⁵⁴Meanwhile, Peter followed him at a distance and went right into the high priest's courtyard. There he sat with the guards, warming himself by the fire.

⁵⁵Inside, the leading priests and the entire high council[74] were trying to find evidence against Jesus, so they could put him to death. But they couldn't find any. ⁵⁶Many false witnesses spoke against him, but they contradicted each other. ⁵⁷Finally, some men stood up and gave this false testimony: ⁵⁸"We heard him say, 'I will destroy this Temple made with human hands, and in three days I will build another, made without human hands.'" ⁵⁹But even then they didn't get their stories straight!

⁶⁰Then the high priest stood up before the others and asked Jesus, "Well, aren't you going to answer these charges? What do you have to say for yourself?" ⁶¹But Jesus was silent and made no reply. Then the high priest asked him, "Are you the Messiah, the Son of the Blessed One?"

⁶²Jesus said, "I Aм.[75] And you will see the Son of Man seated in the place of power at God's right hand[76] and coming on the clouds of heaven.[77]"

⁶³Then the high priest tore his clothing to show his horror and said, "Why do we need other witnesses? ⁶⁴You have all heard his blasphemy. What is your verdict?"

"Guilty!" they all cried. "He deserves to die!"

⁶⁵Then some of them began to spit at him, and they blindfolded him and beat him with their fists. "Prophesy to us," they jeered. And the guards slapped him as they took him away.

⁶⁶Meanwhile, Peter was in the courtyard below. One of the servant girls who worked for the high priest came by ⁶⁷and noticed Peter warming himself at the fire. She looked at him closely and said, "You were one of those with Jesus of Nazareth.[78]"

---

⁷⁴**14:55** Greek *the Sanhedrin.*
⁷⁵**14:62a** Or *The 'I Aм' is here;* or *I am the Lord.* See Exod 3:14.
⁷⁶**14:62b** Greek *at the right hand of the power.* See Ps 110:1.
⁷⁷**14:62c** See Dan 7:13.
⁷⁸**14:67** Or *Jesus the Nazarene.*

[68]But Peter denied it. "I don't know what you're talking about," he said, and he went out into the entryway. Just then, a rooster crowed.[79]

[69]When the servant girl saw him standing there, she began telling the others, "This man is definitely one of them!" [70]But Peter denied it again.

A little later some of the other bystanders confronted Peter and said, "You must be one of them, because you are a Galilean."

[71]Peter swore, "A curse on me if I'm lying—I don't know this man you're talking about!" [72]And immediately the rooster crowed the second time.

Suddenly, Jesus' words flashed through Peter's mind: "Before the rooster crows twice, you will deny three times that you even know me." And he broke down and wept.

[15:1]Very early in the morning the leading priests, the elders, and the teachers of religious law—the entire high council[80]—met to discuss their next step. They bound Jesus, led him away, and took him to Pilate, the Roman governor.

[2]Pilate asked Jesus, "Are you the king of the Jews?"

Jesus replied, "You have said it."

[3]Then the leading priests kept accusing him of many crimes, [4]and Pilate asked him, "Aren't you going to answer them? What about all these charges they are bringing against you?" [5]But Jesus said nothing, much to Pilate's surprise.

[6]Now it was the governor's custom each year during the Passover celebration to release one prisoner—anyone the people requested. [7]One of the prisoners at that time was Barabbas, a revolutionary who had committed murder in an uprising. [8]The crowd went to Pilate and asked him to release a prisoner as usual.

[9]"Would you like me to release to you this 'King of the Jews'?" Pilate asked. [10](For he realized by now that the leading priests had arrested Jesus out of envy.) [11]But at this point the leading priests stirred up the crowd to demand the release of Barabbas instead of Jesus. [12]Pilate asked them, "Then what should I do with this man you call the king of the Jews?"

[13]They shouted back, "Crucify him!"

[14]"Why?" Pilate demanded. "What crime has he committed?"

But the mob roared even louder, "Crucify him!"

[15]So to pacify the crowd, Pilate released Barabbas to them. He ordered Jesus flogged with a lead-tipped whip, then turned him over to the Roman soldiers to be crucified.

[16]The soldiers took Jesus into the courtyard of the governor's headquarters (called the Praetorium) and called out the entire regiment. [17]They dressed him in a purple robe, and they wove thorn branches into a crown and put it on his head. [18]Then they saluted him and taunted, "Hail! King of the Jews!" [19]And they struck him on the head with a reed stick, spit on him, and dropped to their

---

[79] **14:68** Some manuscripts do not include *Just then, a rooster crowed.*
[80] **15:1** Greek *the Sanhedrin*; also in 15:43.

knees in mock worship. ²⁰When they were finally tired of mocking him, they took off the purple robe and put his own clothes on him again. Then they led him away to be crucified.

²¹A passerby named Simon, who was from Cyrene,[81] was coming in from the countryside just then, and the soldiers forced him to carry Jesus' cross. (Simon was the father of Alexander and Rufus.) ²²And they brought Jesus to a place called Golgotha (which means "Place of the Skull"). ²³They offered him wine drugged with myrrh, but he refused it.

²⁴Then the soldiers nailed him to the cross. They divided his clothes and threw dice[82] to decide who would get each piece. ²⁵It was nine o'clock in the morning when they crucified him. ²⁶A sign announced the charge against him. It read, "The King of the Jews." ²⁷Two revolutionaries[83] were crucified with him, one on his right and one on his left.[84]

²⁹The people passing by shouted abuse, shaking their heads in mockery. "Ha! Look at you now!" they yelled at him. "You said you were going to destroy the Temple and rebuild it in three days. ³⁰Well then, save yourself and come down from the cross!"

³¹The leading priests and teachers of religious law also mocked Jesus. "He saved others," they scoffed, "but he can't save himself! ³²Let this Messiah, this King of Israel, come down from the cross so we can see it and believe him!" Even the men who were crucified with Jesus ridiculed him.

³³At noon, darkness fell across the whole land until three o'clock. ³⁴Then at three o'clock Jesus called out with a loud voice, *"Eloi, Eloi, lema sabachthani?"* which means "My God, my God, why have you abandoned me?"[85]

³⁵Some of the bystanders misunderstood and thought he was calling for the prophet Elijah. ³⁶One of them ran and filled a sponge with sour wine, holding it up to him on a reed stick so he could drink. "Wait!" he said. "Let's see whether Elijah comes to take him down!"

³⁷Then Jesus uttered another loud cry and breathed his last. ³⁸And the curtain in the sanctuary of the Temple was torn in two, from top to bottom.

³⁹When the Roman officer[86] who stood facing him[87] saw how he had died, he exclaimed, "This man truly was the Son of God!"

⁴⁰Some women were there, watching from a distance, including Mary Magdalene, Mary (the mother of James the younger and of Joseph[88]), and Salome. ⁴¹They had been followers of Jesus and had cared for him while he was in Galilee. Many other women who had come with him to Jerusalem were also there.

---

[81] **15:21** *Cyrene* was a city in northern Africa.
[82] **15:24** Greek *cast lots.* See Ps 22:18.
[83] **15:27a** Or *Two criminals.*
[84] **15:27b** Some manuscripts add verse 28, *And the Scripture was fulfilled that said, "He was counted among those who were rebels."* See Isa 53:12; also compare Luke 22:37.
[85] **15:34** Ps 22:1.
[86] **15:39a** Greek *the centurion;* similarly in 15:44, 45.
[87] **15:39b** Some manuscripts add *heard his cry and.*
[88] **15:40** Greek *Joses;* also in 15:47. See Matt 27:56.

⁴²This all happened on Friday, the day of preparation,[89] the day before the Sabbath. As evening approached, ⁴³Joseph of Arimathea took a risk and went to Pilate and asked for Jesus' body. (Joseph was an honored member of the high council, and he was waiting for the Kingdom of God to come.) ⁴⁴Pilate couldn't believe that Jesus was already dead, so he called for the Roman officer and asked if he had died yet. ⁴⁵The officer confirmed that Jesus was dead, so Pilate told Joseph he could have the body. ⁴⁶Joseph bought a long sheet of linen cloth. Then he took Jesus' body down from the cross, wrapped it in the cloth, and laid it in a tomb that had been carved out of the rock. Then he rolled a stone in front of the entrance. ⁴⁷Mary Magdalene and Mary the mother of Joseph saw where Jesus' body was laid.

---

[89] **15:42** Greek *It was the day of preparation.*

Tesserae

A Map for the Mosaic

A mosaic is made up of many small pieces of marble, glass, or tile called "tesserae." This devotional is adapted from *Holy Bible: Mosaic*, which is made up of hundreds of tesserae, the words and art of believers from throughout the centuries and across the globe. Each piece is taken from a larger whole, and these pages are a roadmap to guide you in tracking down each piece in its original context.

Lent, Week 1: Identifying Discontent
Pablo Sanaguano Sanchez (Ecuador/Contemporary), *Via Crucis*, 1994. Missio Internationales Katholisches Missionswerk.
E. M. Bounds (USA/1835–1913), *Satan: His Personality, Power, and Overthrow*, Chapter 6.
John Charles Ryle (England/1816–1900), *Thoughts for Young Men*.
Watchman Nee (China/1903–1972), *The Normal Christian Life* (1977).
Frederick Ohler (USA/Contemporary), *Better than Nice and Other Unconventional Prayers* (1989).
Eileen Button, "Hollow Sacrifice."
César Chávez (USA/1927–1993), "Prayer for the Farmworkers' Struggle."

Lent, Week 2: Dependence
Ben Shahn (USA/1898–1969), *Ex-Farmer and Child, Now on WPA*, 1938. Library of Congress, Prints & Photographs Division, FSA-OWI Collection, LC-DIG-fsa-8a18443.
William Ralph Inge (USA/1860–1964), *The Philosophy of Plotinus*.
John Cassian (Egypt/c. 365–435), *Conferences of John Cassian*.
Dietrich Bonhoeffer (Germany/1906–1945), *Letters and Papers from Prison* (1953).
Cyprian (Tunisia/d. 258), *Treatises*, Treatise IV.14.
Karen Sloan, "Lean on Me."

Lent, Week 3: God's Holiness and Grace
Hatigammana Uttarananda (Sri Lanka/Contemporary), *Woman at the Well*, 2000. Missio Internationales Katholisches Missionswerk.
Karl Barth (Switzerland/1886–1968), *Church Dogmatics II.1* (1957).
Augustine of Hippo (Algeria/354–430), "Prayer to the Holy Spirit."
Keith Potter, "Holy God."
Jonathan Edwards (USA/1703–1758), *A Treatise Concerning Religious Affections*, Part 3, Chapter 1.
Yusufu Turaki (Nigeria/Contemporary), *Africa Bible Commentary* (2006).

Lent, Week 4: Sin and Death
Fra Angelico (Italy/c. 1395–1455), *The Crucified Christ*, c. 1442.
Pandita Ramabai (India/1858–1922), qtd. in Helen S. Dyer, *Pandita Ramabai: The Story of Her Life* (1900), Chapter 7.
George Herbert (England/1593–1633), "The Sacrifice."
F. B. Meyer (England/1847–1929), "For Pardon and Power to Do."

Timothy G. Walton, "The Smell of Sin."
Book of Common Prayer (England/1662).
Jan Hus (Bohemia/c. 1369–1415), *Exposition of the Faith.*

Lent, Week 5: Fasting
Fray Gabriel Chavez and Jaime Domínguez Montes (Mexico/Contemporary), *Última Cena*, 1996 (www.arcorbe.org).
Didache (c. 90–180) 8:1-3.
Lauren F. Winner (USA/Contemporary), *Mudhouse Sabbath* (2007).
John Calvin (France/1509–1564), *Institutes of the Christian Religion* 4.12.15.
Donald S. Whitney (USA/Contemporary).
Ole Hallesby (Norway/1879–1961), *Prayer* (1931).
Clyde Taber, "Purposeful Fasting."
Akanu Ibaim (Nigeria/1906–1995), "Fear of the Unknown" in Desmond Tutu, *An African Prayer Book* (1996).

Passion Week: Hope
Valerie Sjodin (USA/Contemporary), *Cleansing Flow*, 2007.
Adam R. Holz (USA/Contemporary), *Discipleship Journal*.
Watchman Nee (China/1903–1972), *The Normal Christian Life* (1977).
Augustine of Hippo (Algeria/354–430), *Confessions*, Book 4, Chapter 16.
George MacDonald (Scotland/1824–1905), *Annals of a Quiet Neighborhood*, "Sermon on God and Mammon."
Book of Common Prayer (England/1662).
Steve Thomason, "Saturday."